TED DIBIASE

The Million Dollar Man

TED DIBIASE

The Million Dollar Man

Ted DiBiase with Tom Caiazzo

Foreword by Jim "J.R." Ross

Special Foreword by Terry Funk

Pocket Books

World Wrestling Entertainment®

NEW YORK   LONDON   TORONTO   SYDNEY

Pocket Books
A Division of Simon & Schuster, Inc.
1230 Avenue of the Americas
New York, NY 10020

First Pocket Books trade paperback edition June 2008

POCKET and colophon are registered trademarks of Simon & Schuster, Inc.

For information about special discounts for bulk purchases,
please contact Simon & Schuster Special Sales at 1-800-456-6798
or business@simonandschuster.com.

Designed by Ruth Lee-Mui

Manufactured in the United States of America

10 9 8 7 6 5 4 3 2 1

ISBN-13: 978-1-4165-5890-3
ISBN-10:   1-4165-5890-X

To

 **MELANIE**

the best-looking girl at the pool, for sure!!

CONTENTS

FOREWORD

Ted DiBiase may be known as the Million Dollar Man to wrestling fans around the world, but to me he will always be known as simply Teddy.

You see, Teddy and I have known each other for over thirty years, ever since we first got into the sports entertainment business in the midseventies, when we both got our "bachelor's degree" in Wrestling 101 from the same man, "Cowboy" Bill Watts, in the Mid-South territory. Subsequently, we both received our "advanced degrees" in the business from Vince McMahon in World Wrestling Federation. In between, we both had gone on quite a journey, especially Theodore—or Marvin, as "Captain Redneck" Dick Murdoch used to call the man most people know as the Million Dollar Man.

Ted DiBiase is one of the best in-ring performers I've ever seen or ever will see. As a second-generation wrestler whose mom *and* stepfather were both pro wrestlers back in the day, young Teddy was a student of the game from day one and always seemed to be a natural fit for "the business." However, the business, especially during the territory days, oftentimes gobbled up young wrestlers and spit them back out as not-so-changed-for-the-better human beings. The temptations of the road were many, and were often overwhelming for young men who were just starting their adult lives. There was plenty of sex, drugs, and rock 'n' roll in the wrestling territories back in the seventies, and Ted DiBiase was not immune to these temptations. Neither was I, as best I remember, but somehow we both survived our miraculous journey through the scandalous seventies and the excesses of the eighties.

Ted's story of his life in the wrestling business goes from his early days as a young and impressionable man in a wild and woolly territory—working for a demanding, albeit brilliant boss—to his ascent to the top of the sports entertainment world, working for the most powerful man in the history of the business. Ted's "excellent adventure" documents his interactions with some of the most famous individuals of all time in the sports entertainment field, including: Andre the Giant, Ric Flair, Hulk Hogan, and, of course, Ted's mentor, Dick Murdoch, to name just a few of the legends you will read about through the eyes of one of the most prominent and important figures in the history of what is perhaps the most unique, maligned, and controversial business imaginable.

These stories must be read to be believed, and through the grace of God, Ted DiBiase is still here to tell of his amazing experience in the wrestling and sports entertainment business, one that will never be duplicated. The life's journey of the Million Dollar Man is pure gold.

—Jim "J.R." Ross

SPECIAL FOREWORD

I had three mentors in the world of professional wrestling: my father, Eddie Graham, and "Iron" Mike DiBiase. All three men were wonderful people, and they taught me so much about the business. Unfortunately, Mike died from a heart attack in the prime of his life. Because of all the things he had done for me, I wanted to do something for his son, Teddy. Initially, it had nothing to do with the wrestling business; I was more concerned with helping Teddy get an education. Although he was offered a football scholarship at the University of Arizona, I steered him to West Texas State University. While I wanted to make sure he finished college and earned his degree, I also wanted Teddy in Canyon for selfish reasons: so that I could watch him play football.

What I didn't realize about Teddy was that he came to West Texas State not only to play football and get a degree, but also to pursue a career in professional wrestling. At the time, West Texas State had produced some of the best wrestlers in the country, including those who had worked in the Amarillo territory: Bruiser Brody, Stan Hansen, Dory Funk Jr., Ray Stevens, Pat Patterson, Tito Santana, Tully Blanchard, Dick Murdoch, Dusty Rhodes, and me, among others. When he decided to leave college early and pursue wrestling full-time, I was upset: I wanted him to finish his studies. But he was in love with the business and knew exactly what he was doing.

Wrestling was in Teddy's genes. His mother, Helen Hild, was one of the best and most beautiful women workers there was in the business. His stepfather was one of the greatest in-ring wrestlers and was also an incredible athlete at the University of Nebraska. Following their lead, Teddy had come to the right place to learn his craft. While in Amarillo, he learned to respect the business and made a commitment to do extremely well. Through his dedication and because he came into the business properly, Teddy became one of the truly great performers in the history of professional wrestling. He had an insatiable love for the business—maybe at times he loved it too much—and I don't think there could have been a better Million Dollar Man.

Teddy still has a lot to offer to professional wrestling. But he also has a great deal to offer to the layperson, someone who may be walking through this world needing to understand God a little better.

Teddy is an honest person and has a huge heart. In business and in life, he has never tried to manipulate or take advantage of anyone. I still call Teddy a kid, because that's what he will always be to me. I love him like he was one of my own. My life, as well as the world of professional wrestling, is much better because of Ted DiBiase.

—Terry Funk

TED DIBIASE

1

FORCED TO RETIRE

In 1993, my last wrestling match in the United States was at *SummerSlam* in Detroit against Razor Ramon. I could have stayed as long as I wanted in World Wrestling Federation; Vince McMahon and everyone in the company had treated me with the utmost respect. But the travel schedule was wearing on me and I wanted to spend more time at home with my family. I missed my wife and my three sons, Michael, Teddy Jr., and Brett. So I chose to leave to pursue other wrestling opportunities.

After taking a few weeks off to rejuvenate, I lined up some bookings with Sohei "Giant" Baba's All-Japan promotion. I first met Baba when I was playing college football at West Texas State; Terry Funk introduced me to him after a match in Amarillo. When I got into wrestling, Giant Baba invited me to work for a four-week tour, and I continued to work for him over the next two decades.

The schedule in Japan was lighter and I would be able to spend a lot more time with my family. Baba also gave me a great financial deal. Besides the money, I was issued round-trip first-class airfare and guaranteed all accommodations. The only thing I had to pay for was my food.

My first night back in Japan, I was immediately teamed up with my good friend and West Texas State alum Stan Hansen. Stan was the most popular American wrestler in all of Japan. Even though it was my first trip back since 1987, I was put right to work in the main events. My first match was in the Budokan in Tokyo; in front of thirty thousand fans, we captured the tag-team titles.

During the match, I took a basic bump. When I landed, a razor-sharp pain shot down both my arms. I got up and immediately tagged in Stan, and he could tell something was wrong. But somehow, through the pain, I managed to finish the match and we became the new champions.

The pain subsided and didn't return until after about three more matches. After I took a simple body slam, the sharp twinges once again pulsed down my arms, and the pain continued for the next few weeks. All I could think of was finishing out the tour, but the pain was getting worse. The bottom line was that I knew something wasn't right. So I finished the three-week tour and headed home.

A few days later, I went to see my local doctor. He referred me to the best neurosurgeon in the state of Mississippi, Dr. Glenn Warren. He ran some tests and scheduled me for an MRI. The results showed that I had two herniated cervical disks in the base of my neck, which was where I had landed when taking the bump. Dr. Warren said, "Ted, you have two choices. Undergo surgery, which would consist of some dissection of your muscle and tissue, and a bone graft procedure, or try a course of rehabilitation using a traction machine.

"Either way, I suggest you retire from professional wrestling." I was blown away. Sensing my disbelief, he added, "The pain is just going to get worse. You can try the traction, but inevitably you are going to need the surgery. And even after the surgery, if you get dropped on the area just right, you could be paralyzed for life or even killed." I was stunned. I understood what he was saying, but I couldn't believe it. At the time, I guess I just didn't want to go through what I thought was unneeded surgery.

I also was in denial. At this point, I needed to get my life back on track. For years, due to World Wrestling Federation's demanding road schedule, I'd conducted myself in a very immoral and unprincipled manner. Not only was I drinking and using drugs, I was unfaithful in my marriage. Although I'd been happily married to Melanie for more than a decade, my overinflated ego led me to womanizing.

In 1993, shortly before *WrestleMania IX,* Melanie found out about this behavior. I begged for her forgiveness; the thought of losing everything that I loved—my wife and children—scared me to death. Luckily for me, Melanie agreed to give me a second chance. In the interest of saving my marriage, I decided that wrestling in Japan was the best thing to do.

Needless to say, I was very concerned. Giant Baba had just given me a generous contract and I needed the money to support my family. Before I left the doctor's office, I explained my situation to him. I told him I had to go back and give it a try out of respect to both Baba and my career.

So, I chose the rehabilitation. The doctor gave me this traction device, which I was required to wear for about thirty minutes a day. A week or so later, I packed the device with my bags and headed back to Japan for another three-week tour.

After only three days in Japan, I was in so much pain that I couldn't wrestle. The next evening, I spoke to Giant Baba in the dressing room. I respectfully explained to him the entire situation and that I needed to go home to have the surgery. Baba knew exactly what I was talking about—it turned out he had the same medical condition. He told me that he would meet me at my hotel in the morning to pay me for my three days of work.

That next morning, Baba told me that I was welcome back to All-Japan anytime. He then opened a briefcase full of cash. I was expecting him to pay me for only the three days, but Baba proceeded to count out all the money he had guaranteed me for the entire three-week tour. I was flabbergasted. Baba was all class, and the gesture showed me just how much he respected me. We shook hands and I left for the airport to catch my plane back home.

Although I put surgery off for a few more years, I took the doctor's advice and never wrestled anywhere again. When I went back to work for Vince as a commentator and manager, and even later as a producer, I never wrestled. I wasn't taking any bumps, so I didn't think I needed surgery. I kept holding off because I thought I could tolerate the pain, and also that the rehab would ease the pain. But nothing worked, and at times the pain was unbearable.

It wasn't until 1996 that I checked into the River Oaks Hospital in Jackson, Mississippi, for my herniated cervical disk surgery. After I was prepped and had my vitals checked, I was given anesthesia. The doctor proceeded to remove a portion of the herniated disk that was pushing on the nerve. He made an incision in the front of my neck in order to reach the spine, then removed disk material from the nerve and fused it with two bone plugs taken from my hip. Some four hours later, I woke up in the recovery room. I spent only one night in the hospital, but it took me about a week to recover. Although the surgery was a success, the scars on my hip and on my neck are a daily reminder of the incident that eventually forced me into retirement.

2

WORLD WRESTLING FEDERATION CHAMPION—NOT REALLY

Technically, I didn't win the World Wrestling Federation Heavyweight Championship.

In June of 1987, shortly after the conclusion of *WrestleMania III*, my Million Dollar Man character was introduced to the world via a series of video vignettes. These were crafted in such a manner that even before I stepped into a World Wrestling Federation ring, the fans

couldn't stand me. For example, one vignette showed me riding in a stretch limousine. With my personal bodyguard, Virgil, by my side, I stepped out of the vehicle and said arrogantly, "Hello, I'm Ted DiBiase. I'm the Million Dollar Man."

Another vignette showed me using my vast amount of money to gain favors and special treatment. I went to a public swimming pool, where kids were playing and enjoying themselves. I decided that I wanted to swim and have the pool all to myself. I called over the pool attendant and told him that I needed my privacy and that all the kids had to get out. Of course, the pool attendant said, "I can't kick everyone out of a public pool, especially not the kids." I said, "Look, you don't understand. I am the Million Dollar Man. I don't wait on anybody." I called Virgil with a snap of my fingers, and he pulled out a wad of money, handing the pool guy four or five hundred dollars. The pool attendant took the money and said, "I think there is too much chlorine in the water. I'll be right back." The next thing you saw was Virgil kicking all the kids out one by one, and me sitting on a lounge chair in my bathing suit, enjoying the pool, while all the kids were staring at me with sad faces from outside the fence. Then I turned to the camera and said, "Don't get upset with the pool guy. He's no different than you. He did the same thing that anybody would do. He took the money. Just like him, everybody has a price for the Million Dollar Man."

I would always conclude these vignettes by turning to the camera, grinning with sheer evil, and stating, "You see, *everybody* has their price for the Million Dollar Man."

All these vignettes were designed to fuel the fans' anger, but it was a live event at the MECCA arena in Milwaukee that really catapulted my character to the hated status. In another effort to show my evil side, and that everyone had a price, I offered a five-year-old boy an opportunity to win some money. I asked the eager child, "Can you bounce a basketball?"

"Yes," he replied.

"Can you bounce it ten times in a row?"

"Uh-huh," he answered.

Virgil lifted the boy from the ringside-seat area and took him into the ring. The cute-as-could-be young man easily dribbled the ball ten consecutive times. With the crowd sensing my compassion, I said, "That's great. Now, if you can bounce the ball fifteen times in a row, I'll give you five hundred dollars."

With the crowd cheering the young boy on, he dribbled away. After his fourteenth dribble, I stuck out my foot, which caused him to miss the last bounce. As the crowd gasped in disbelief, the little boy started to cry, and I told him, "Ah, you missed, how unfortunate for you, son. You are going to learn a very hard lesson at a very young age. When you don't get the job done, you don't get paid!" I laughed. The young boy burst into tears and ran to his mother.

BRUCE PRICHARD (Brother Love):

We had so much fun with the creation of Ted's vignettes. They were real and everyone involved got their money. More important, they accomplished our goal of introducing to the wrestling world the Million Dollar Man character.

I was now a full-fledged heel and my character was established as a person who could buy anything he wanted. In fact, I proclaimed the unthinkable: I told the fans that I was going to buy the World Wrestling Federation heavyweight title. To help me with this transaction, I was going to contract out Andre the Giant to beat the champion, Hulk Hogan. After Andre defeated Hogan, I would purchase the title from Andre. Since he was cheated out of the title by Hogan at *WrestleMania III*, Andre enthusiastically agreed to my terms.

The stage was set for February 5, 1988. The night was a historic one, because it was the first time professional wrestling was being broadcast on live national network television since the 1950s. During the event, which aired during prime time on NBC as part of a special *The Main Event*, Hulk Hogan was set to defend his title against Andre the Giant. Of course, since I had purchased Andre's services, I was going to be ringside.

What followed was probably one of the greatest angles and finishes of all time.

In a rematch from *WrestleMania III* and as the setup for *WrestleMania IV*, Hulk Hogan dominated the match. With my investment in trouble, I continually fussed and demanded that Andre win my title. Toward the end of the match, referee Dave Hebner got trapped between Hogan and Andre, and was knocked out cold. I quickly dragged Hebner out of the ring and signaled for a new referee. The crowd totally freaked out when none other than Dave Hebner's identical twin brother, Earl, became the new referee.

Unbeknownst to the crowd, and due to my influence and money, Earl was Dave's "evil" twin. Andre quickly recovered and gave Hogan a huge body slam, then went to pin Hogan. Even though Hogan had one shoulder up, Earl counted "one-two-three" and called for the bell declaring Andre the new champion. The crowd was stunned! Hogan was furious and despite his plea, Earl proceeded to call for the championship belt. We entered the ring, and he raised Andre's hand in victory. Andre was then given the championship belt.

With a smile as large as life, Andre showed me the belt, then put it around my waist and declared me the new heavyweight champion. With my hand raised in victory, I was on top of the world.

All of a sudden, Dave Hebner regained consciousness and reentered the ring. He argued with Earl about the match result. Andre and I rolled out of the ring as the two brothers argued. Meanwhile, Hogan was still steaming over the obvious con job and grabbed both men by their shirts. He glanced back and forth between them in disbelief. Everyone in the crowd, as well as Hogan, was stunned by what had just occurred. Nobody saw it coming.

BRUCE PRICHARD:

Ted's purchase of the heavyweight title from Andre was a history-making event. We kept it real quiet and nobody knew about it except the talents involved. The goal of the angle was threefold: (1) to get a Hulk Hogan and Andre the Giant rematch; (2) to move the Million Dollar Man character into the spotlight; and, (3) to plant the seed for the introduction of Ted's Million Dollar Belt.

I wrestled as the "champion" for some two weeks; however, my champion status would soon be challenged and questioned. The president of World Wrestling Federation, Jack Tunney, issued a proclamation: he was taking the title away from me.

President Tunney was in a sticky situation. He couldn't give the title back to Hulk Hogan, because technically he lost the match against Andre. Andre wouldn't take the title because I had paid him off. And I couldn't keep

the title because I didn't win it legitimately. The solution was to have a tournament at *WrestleMania IV* to declare a new champion.

WrestleMania IV was my first *WrestleMania*. The event was held at the Trump Plaza in Atlantic City, New Jersey, on March 27, 1988; Donald Trump himself was in attendance.

I wrestled three times that night. In the first round of the tournament, with both Andre and Virgil by my side, I pinned "Hacksaw" Jim Duggan. In my quarterfinal match, I wrestled and pinned Don "the Rock" Muraco. Because I had interfered in Hulk Hogan and Andre the Giant's quarterfinal match, causing both men to be eliminated, I didn't have an opponent in the semifinal, so I was now in the finals against fellow heel Randy "Macho Man" Savage.

During the course of the match, Andre attacked Randy outside the ring. Sensing trouble, Randy's manager, Miss Elizabeth, ran to the back. Within a few minutes, the crowd went wild as she returned with none other than Hulk Hogan. Now it was Andre in my corner and Hogan in Randy's. Even though

Randy was a heel, the crowd could feel his babyface turn with each passing minute of the match.

In the end, I had Randy in my finishing move, the Million Dollar Dream. Elizabeth got up on the ring apron and distracted the referee. Hulk Hogan entered the ring and nailed me in the back with a steel chair. Soon thereafter, the Macho Man pinned me after dropping his patented flying elbow drop from the top rope. Randy Savage was crowned the new champion.

Although I lost the title, I was still very arrogant and quite rich. I told everyone that the world heavyweight title didn't matter. I didn't need the title. Rather, I created my own belt: the Million Dollar Belt. From that day forward, I became the self-proclaimed Million Dollar Champion, crowing and bragging that my belt was worth millions of dollars in gold and diamonds.

BRUCE PRICHARD:

The Million Dollar Man character was perfect for Ted. His skills in the ring were excellent, and he played the character to perfection. He carried himself like he owned the world—just the way we envisioned.

For more than three decades, I have been a part of professional wrestling and have literally done it all, traveling all over the world, including to Australia, Europe, and Japan. I have been to all fifty states. I have wrestled alone and as part of a tag team, and I've served as a referee, a manager, an announcer, a producer, and an advisor to the creative team.

I have held almost every title in the business and have worked for every major promotion. Some of my accomplishments include: AJPW International Heavyweight Champion (four times); NWA National Heavyweight Champion; NWA National Tag Team Champion (two times); Mid-South North American Heavyweight Champion (four times) and Mid-South Tag Team Champion (four times); World Wrestling Federation World Tag Team Champion (three times); and the *King of the Ring 1988*.

Not too bad for someone who technically didn't win the title.

That's me riding the streets of Willcox.

3

THE EARLY YEARS

On January 18, 1954, at 11:11 p.m., I was born two months premature to Ted Wills and Gladys Helen Nevins in Miami Beach, Florida. I weighed in at five pounds, eleven ounces.

My dad, whom I was named after, was born and raised in South Florida, and was an entertainer and singer. He had a great bass voice and was a regular on *The Tennessee Ernie Ford Show.*

My mother was born in Grand Island, Nebraska. She was

extremely attractive and was a great dancer. In her early years, she worked as a showgirl, performing with many of the big bands of the 1940s and with Frank Sinatra.

At sixteen years old, she married her first husband, professional wrestler "Spiderman" Al Galento. She was clearly too young, and the marriage was doomed from the start. When she discovered that Al had had an affair, my mom divorced him (she was pregnant with my older brother, Albert Jr., at the time). The marriage lasted less than six months.

After the divorce, her parents, Edgar and Marie Nevins, helped out with raising Albert. At the time, my grandparents were living in Omaha, Nebraska, and were in the restaurant business. One day, my grandma read an advertisement in the paper about a local café for sale in Willcox, Arizona. The deal was too good to pass up; plus, her doctor recommended that she move somewhere warmer to help her arthritis. So, with my mom and Albert, my grandparents moved west to run Marie's Truck Stop Café.

With my older brother in good hands, my mother went back on the road, and it was while she was touring that she met and fell in love with my father.

I didn't get much of a chance to build a life with my parents, since they were always gone, and when I was two years old, Ted and my mother got a divorce. During my toddler years, my grandmother raised Michael and me (Albert had legally changed his name to Michael after our mom married Mike DiBiase).

I don't have too many childhood memories of Ted. But I do remember one time that he came for a visit when I was four years old. My mother was on the road. Ted asked me if I wanted to go on a trip with him to Los Angeles. He said, "If we use our time wisely, I imagine we can even sneak in a trip to Disneyland."

I really wanted to go to Disneyland with my dad, but it was up to my grandmother. She adored Ted and thought he was a great guy, so she didn't see any harm in him taking me. "I don't think there would be any problem with the two of you spending time together," she'd said. As quick as I could, I packed my stuff and, together with my dad, I headed west to California.

It was a wonderful and unforgettable trip. My dad showed me the town, fed me great food, and, as promised, took me to Disneyland. He even took me to see the movie *Sleeping Beauty*. After the movie, we got something to eat and headed to the toy store. We walked in and went straight to the *Sleeping Beauty* toy display. I was overwhelmed. Dad bought me a little plastic sword and shield just like the prince had in the movie. As an added bonus, he bought me the *Sleeping Beauty* children's storybook to read later. I was so happy!

I also got a chance to watch my dad perform onstage. I remember him rehearsing his part as a backup singer for Tennessee Ernie Ford. He even introduced me to Mr. Ford. After shaking my hand, Mr. Ford told my dad, "Bring him out to the house this weekend. My wife will just love this kid!"

On Sunday afternoon, me with my *Sleeping Beauty* toys and book in hand, Dad drove us into the hills of Hollywood to Mr. Ford's luxurious home. His estate was huge, with a giant swimming pool in the backyard. It was the first time I had seen a television on the ceiling of a bedroom. I had a great time and ate a wonderful meal. Ernie's wife was super nice, and I can still remember crawling up onto her lap as she read *Sleeping Beauty* to me.

Just as I was starting to bond with Ted, my vacation unexpectedly ended. Mom had come home early. When my grandmother explained where I was, she was livid, I mean steaming mad. She immediately took the next flight from Tucson to Los Angeles, and it seemed like just as I hugged my mom upon her arrival, I was back in Willcox.

I don't think my dad meant anything bad by taking me to California, but my mother was angry because he didn't ask her permission. It would be the last time I saw Ted for quite some time.

When I was older, I asked my mother why she and Ted divorced. "It wasn't that Ted was a bad guy. He didn't beat me or anything like that. But I so wanted to feel secure. Ted didn't meet that need for me. He had talent but no ambition. He was the kind of guy who would sit back waiting for the big break to come to him, rather than going out looking to make it happen. He was just too carefree for me."

I later found out that Ted was approached by a major producer to take a part as a singing cowboy in a huge country-and-western television program.

Ted thought the idea was ridiculous and turned down the part. He didn't want to have anything to do with the show. Well, that "ridiculous" singing cowboy part went instead to Roy Rogers. I'm sure there were no happy trails for Ted after that.

After the divorce, Mom continued to make her living on the road. However, she made a career change and was no longer a showgirl. She chose a profession that was more physically demanding, where beauty was just as important as strength. Mom entered the professional wrestling circuit.

BOB GEIGEL:

Helen was a very good wrestler. She was also quite attractive. I first met Teddy in 1957 when he was traveling with his mother. She was wrestling in Tucson. When he was three years old, I taught Teddy how to swim in the hotel's swimming pool.

Women's wrestling was a very glamorous and thrilling profession. Besides my mother, there were other beautiful and very athletic female wrestlers in that era, including the Fabulous Moolah, Mae Young, Vickie Williams, Toni Rose, Susan Green, and Joyce Grable.

Since the road was no place for kids, my brother Mike and I stayed with my grandparents in Willcox. I loved living with my grandparents. Willcox was one of those dust-blown towns located on Interstate 10 between Phoenix and El Paso, Texas. I remember there was only one stoplight and one paved road. Even now, it has fewer than five thousand people.

Things weren't like they are today, when you have to keep an eye on your child every second. I distinctly remember walking and riding my bike all over town by myself at five years old. I would walk to and from school with my mutt dog Curly (my grandfather called him Blacky).

I was a good student, so as a reward my grandmother would often give me fifty cents to go into town and watch a movie. The movie theater was only about two miles from the café. I would ride my bike down Railroad Avenue to

My mom wrestled as Helen Hild.

the theater. I'd pay twenty-five cents to see the movie, ten cents for a Coke, ten cents for a box of popcorn, and a nickel for a candy bar. For fifty cents, I enjoyed the movie and had a feast. Times sure have changed.

I used to walk to the full-service gas station next door to Grandma's café. It was there that I saw diverse people from all over the country. I even helped out the station attendant by cleaning either the car's headlights or windows.

I remember the *Superman* television show was very popular at that time. I, of course, wanted to be just like Superman. I would go get a dish towel from the café's kitchen and have Grandma pin it to the collar on the back of my shirt. When I walked, ran, or rode my bike, the towel would flap in the wind just like my hero's cape.

I hung out with my grandfather, Edgar, who was a retired Union Pacific Railroad engineer. He often took me to school. He was a gentle man and was very magnanimous. I used to enjoy watching him work in the garden.

Grandpa was a diabetic. I would watch him take his insulin shot in the thigh right before breakfast. He would drop his pants right there in the kitchen. He was very careful with his diet because of his condition. Every morning he would get up and have the same thing: soft-boiled eggs, wheat toast, and a bowl of Wheaties or Shredded Wheat.

After lunch, Grandpa would go out to the back porch and smoke a cigar. I was curious and would always ask him if I could smoke his cigar. He would smoke that cigar down to the butt and then give it to me. He'd say, "Now, don't inhale it." I thought it was the coolest thing to puff on that cigar.

Grandpa did some crazy things. I don't know if it was because he was getting up there in age, but he always kept Grandma on her toes. One time, he got this idea that he was going to paint his car. It was a nice, moon-shaped vehicle that ran quite well. He went to the local paint store and purchased a couple of gallons of latex house paint. Right from the can, he painted the entire car silver. My grandma was furious and righty so. The car looked hideous.

My grandmother was an angel. She cared for my brother and me and was very giving and compassionate. I recall many times when she gave hoboes free meals and helped others in need. She was very gracious and taught me about empathy and kindness. Because of her, I have always treated people with dignity and respect.

But Grandma was one tough lady too. Smoking her trademark Salem cigarettes, she would work long hours in the restaurant. As a woman in the 1950s running a truck stop café, you had to have a tremendous amount of determination and good leadership skills. And unequivocally she did.

So many people have told me that my grandma went out of her way to help people. She was an unbelievably kind and hardworking woman. She lived to be eighty-nine years old.

JOHN DIBIASE (brother):

Grandma was a sweet and wonderful lady. She always had a smile on her face and would go out of her way to help people. Many times she would feed people who didn't have any money, or even help those out who didn't have enough money to pay the entire meal tab.

She also took care of Teddy and me like we were her own children. She would protect us and make sure that we had everything that we needed. In her eyes, her grandchildren could never do anything wrong.

Every day, my grandmother would sit at a table near the window of the restaurant and wait for me to get out of school. I would eat lunch at the café every day. In fact, Mike and I would eat most of our meals at the café. We spent many of our days there.

I loved watching my grandma cook and bake, especially when she made fresh cakes, pastries, pies, and cinnamon rolls. She made sure I always had my fill, which was probably why I was a husky kid. From birth until my high school years, I was a chubby butterball.

I helped out the best I could by washing dishes or bussing tables. But my favorite time was just watching and listening to the vast array of people who would come into the café.

JOHN DIBIASE:

Ted was seven years older than me. I remember both of us working in my grandma's truck stop. My grandmother was a hard worker and she often had to clean up after me because I wasn't doing such a good job as the dishwasher. I also remember sitting on top of the roof of the restaurant with Teddy to watch the parades in town.

There was a jukebox in my grandmother's café. I enjoyed listening to music and I used to put my own marked quarters (so it wouldn't cost anything) in the slot to listen to the songs. I had many favorites, including anything by Johnny Cash. But my all-time favorite song was Roy Orbison's "Pretty Woman." Today when I hear that song I'm reminded of that place, the people, and my grandma.

4

LEARNING FROM MY DAD

As I was just finishing up kindergarten, my mother fell in love with the person whom I consider my "true dad," Mike DiBiase. "Iron" Mike was also a professional wrestler and they had met on the road.

Born on Christmas Eve, 1923, Mike was a first-generation Italian American. He was the last of three children born to his father's second wife, Christina. He grew up in Omaha in a traditional Italian, Roman Catholic family. Mike was a champion athlete, lettering in football, track, and wrestling. He was tough as nails.

"Iron" Mike DiBiase, my dad.

In 1942, he was Omaha Tech High School's King of Sports and was named Omaha's Outstanding High School Athlete. Dad's excellence on the football field earned him all-city and all-state honors, and he won the Nebraska state heavyweight championship twice.

After graduating high school, in the midst of World War II, Dad joined the navy. At the time he was the youngest chief petty officer. For part of his tour, he was stationed in Norman, Oklahoma. During that time, he won the

Oklahoma AAU heavyweight wrestling title two years in a row. Dad was later transferred to northern California, where he won the Far Western heavyweight title. Then in April of 1946, he won the AAU national heavyweight wrestling title in New York City.

When his enlistment ended, Dad enrolled at the University of Nebraska. It was there that he lettered four times in wrestling and three times in football. Upon graduation in 1950, he was courted by several professional football teams, including the Chicago Bears. The Bears were in dire need of a tough offense and a defensive lineman like my dad. Unfortunately for football, my dad pursued a career in professional wrestling.

TERRY FUNK:

Mike was one of the greatest athletes ever to come out of the state of Nebraska. He received more letters in track, football, and wrestling at the University of Nebraska than anyone else. He had a real understanding of the business and was a legitimate tough guy.

BOB GEIGEL:

Mike was a roughly 230-pound wrestling machine from Omaha. He played football and wrestled at the University of Nebraska. I was around Mike a lot. He was an excellent worker and always conducted himself as a professional. He never complained about anything.

After Mom and Dad married in October of 1959, we left Willcox for Amarillo. I had just started first grade. Although I missed my grandparents, I was really happy to be with my mother. And Mike loved me as his own, which made the move even better.

It's quite ironic—since my mom was born in Grand Island and Mike in Omaha, which are right next to each other—that they never met until they

were wrestling on the road. Even funnier is that as a kid, my dad delivered papers to her house—they even went to the same grade school.

My dad made sure that nobody ever took advantage of me. I remember my cousin Ray and I would always watch TV together, but if I had a better view he would hit me and push me off the couch to claim the spot. I would then run and tell my mother.

Once, when I was six, Ray pushed me off the couch as usual. This time, I ran to tell my new dad. "Teddy, don't let anybody take advantage of you like that. Now you go back over there and smack him to make sure he never does that to you again." Surprised by his comment, I just looked at him.

Then I marched right back into the living room and smacked Ray right across the face. My cousin started crying. After that, he never pushed me off the couch or hit me again. Dad had just given me my first lesson in defending myself.

Dad always told me not to be a bully and don't start trouble, but when somebody starts trouble with you, finish it. Make sure you win the fight so it doesn't happen again. He also told me his three basic rules that I still live by today and have passed on to my children: (1) Don't ever lie; (2) Don't ever cheat; and (3) Don't ever steal.

One hot Amarillo afternoon, I was playing catch with a couple of girls in the neighborhood. We were playing with a rubber ball. One of us missed the throw and the ball went bouncing into the yard next to us.

In the yard was this ferocious bulldog. Before any of us thought of the danger, one of the girls yelled, "I'll go get it." She scaled the fence and proceeded to pick up the ball. The dog started barking up a storm, causing the little girl to freeze in her tracks. I guess sensing fear, the dog attacked the girl.

I quickly jumped over the fence and grabbed the dog by his two hind legs. With all my strength, I grabbed him and threw him straight over my head. The dog hit the ground and ran away whimpering.

I helped the little girl out of the fence and back to my yard. By then, some parents and other grown-ups had gathered around to help us. Unfortunately, the dog bit a pretty big piece of skin out of her right inner arm. Other than that, she was okay.

The incident became the highlight of my first-grade year in Amarillo. I was considered a hero for saving the little girl. It seemed like wherever I went, people would applaud me for being so heroic. My dad was very proud.

I grew up wanting to be a professional wrestler—just like my dad. Many of the wrestlers would come over to the house. I was in awe of them, especially Danny Plechas. He was my dad's tag-team partner and he would often come to visit and eat dinner with us.

Danny was one tough guy. During one of his matches, a big cowboy-looking fan wearing a brand-new pair of Levi's jeans jumped in the ring.

Maybe he had one too many beers, because the fan landed a blow to the back of Danny's neck. As the fan turned around to leave, Danny grabbed him by the seat of his pants, ripping the end right out of them!

Dad used to host card parties: poker, gin rummy, you name it. The boys would sit around drinking beer and telling stories, sometimes until the wee hours of the morning—guys like the Avenger (Art Nelson), Nick Roberts, Dory Funk Sr., and Bob Orton. One night, I recall my parents consoling a crying Nick. I had never seen a grown man cry so much. I later found out that Nick's wife had committed suicide.

JOHN DiBIASE:

I really liked it when the Avenger (Art Nelson) came to the house. He would often be a guest for dinner. He would wear a mask. I was taught by my dad at an early age to protect the business. And thus I was to never, ever tell anyone the true alias of the Avenger. One day, I slipped up and told some of my friends the initials of the name of the Avenger. I got in lots of trouble by my dad for that mishap.

I have been friends with the Funk family my entire life. I knew them very well. In Amarillo, my dad was always a heel, and Dory and his kids were huge babyfaces. The Funks are well known in Amarillo. Dory worked at a boys' ranch with at-risk kids. He was a steward to the community and rightfully received many accolades for his service.

Almost my entire life, I protected the business. Although we were friends with the Funks, we could never be seen interacting together in public. The business was taken very seriously back then. My dad always told me it was real and I believed it. What happened in the ring was nothing personal, it was just business. Friendships went out the window during a match. Afterward, everything was fine. Dad never smartened me up about the business.

In the fall of 1960, while the rest of the country watched the Nixon-Kennedy debates, I had something far more important going on. I was becoming a big brother. I remember how excited I was when I first saw John, he was so small. Mom let me hold him and I felt so proud.

Back then, wrestling was territorial. You could never stay too long in one region. With my dad being a heel, it seemed like we were living in a different apartment every three months. We moved from Amarillo to Portland, Oregon. I didn't like Portland. Not only was it heavily populated, it seemed like it rained every day. It was also the first time I got in major trouble because of the "dirt-clod incident."

When we moved to Portland, my parents rented a decent two-bedroom apartment. With my older brother Mike now staying with my grandparents in Willcox, a thousand-or-so-square-foot apartment was sufficient for my parents and us two kids. As in most traditional Italian families in the early 1960s, my mother stayed home and took care of the children. Dad wouldn't have it any other way.

One early afternoon, I was out behind the apartment complex playing with a neighbor's girl and throwing dirt clods. I loved throwing dirt clods. I would hurl them in the air or use all my might to toss them a long distance. But what I really liked to do was throw them against the wall. When the clod hit the wall, it would make a *boom* sound. To me it sounded like a bomb exploding. It was so cool.

My parents knew I would throw dirt clods. They would tell me over and over not to throw rocks. I could break a window, hurt somebody, or even hurt myself. But like any other kid, I couldn't resist.

I was slinging dirt clods right and left, at a wall near our apartment. I was also throwing them up as high as I could. All of a sudden, one dirt clod got away, and I accidentally hit the girl I was playing with square in the face. She started crying and screaming. Blood started gushing down her face from a cut on the side of her nose.

The little girl's mother rushed to her side. As she tended to the wound, I apologized in a worried tone. "I'm really sorry, ma'am. Honestly, it was an accident. I didn't mean to hit her."

After calming down her daughter and applying an ice bag as well as a large dose of hugs and kisses, the little girl's mother said, "Its okay, young man. My daughter is going to be just fine." I was relieved and smiled at them.

"However, I think you should go back home and tell your parents what happened. Go ahead and tell them and that will be the end of it."

I started heading home, remembering that my dad and mom had told me not to throw rocks. Granted, I didn't throw any rocks, but I wasn't sure if they would see the difference between a rock and a dirt clod.

I got to the front door of my apartment and decided not to go in. I was very nervous and scared. I also simply didn't know what to say or do. I was sure, though, that I didn't want to go home with my father still there.

I knew that my dad would leave every day after four to go wrestle. So I walked across the street and just waited until after four. I would take my chances with Mom and cry and plead that she wouldn't tell my father.

While I was organizing this plan, the girl's mother decided to make a visit to our residence. The lady asked my mom, "Is Teddy here?"

Mom said, "No. He's not back from playing yet. Why are you looking for him?"

"Because I sent him home to tell you what happened. He promised me that he would tell you." My mom invited the lady in and she told them everything.

Finally, it was after four, so I decided to return home. I walked through the front door and there was my dad. He hadn't left for work. Knowing that I had better act fast, I tried to act as normal as possible. I nonchalantly said, "I'm going down to the park to play."

Dad replied, "Hold on, Teddy. Before you go, is there anything you want to tell us?"

"No."

Knowing that I had just lied, my dad lowered the boom. "Are you sure there isn't anything you want to tell us? Are you sure?"

They gave me every opportunity to tell them. Once again, I said, "No."

Well, that was it. My dad called me over to him. "What did I tell you about lying? How about you tell us how you threw the dirt clod at the girl and hit her in the nose?"

I thought to myself, "Oh my gosh, they found out!"

In an empathetic yet stern manner, Dad asked, "Why didn't you come and tell us?"

I sat down and swallowed hard. "I was scared to come and tell you. You told me not to throw rocks. It was a dirt clod and it was an accident."

"Teddy, I know it was an accident. What have I told you? Don't lie, don't cheat, and don't steal. You lied to the girl's mother and you lied to us. We are not raising you to be a liar."

I felt so bad by disappointing my mom and especially my dad. I was expecting a whipping on the butt with his belt, but it didn't happen. "You need to be punished for your disobedience. I am going to give you a choice. You can either wash the dishes for a week, or be grounded for a week."

I thought about it for a few minutes. I knew that being grounded was the harsher punishment. Since I knew that I disappointed Dad, I felt like I deserved the harder of the two. "I'll be grounded for a week."

He nodded in approval and said, "Okay, that is it."

About halfway through the week, Dad called me over. "Here is what I am going to do. I am very proud of you. I hope you learned a lesson. Don't ever be afraid to tell me anything. Always be honest and truthful. I am going to end your grounding early. I gave you a choice of your punishment and you chose the harder one. And because you did, I am going to let you off early."

My dad may have been tough, but he was also fair.

5

ON THE ROAD

Almost immediately after I completed first grade, we left Portland and headed back to Texas. On the way back to the Lone Star State, we stopped to stay with my grandparents in Willcox. It was so nice to see everyone; I'd really missed them a lot. We also got a pleasant surprise. My brother Mike, who was living with our grandparents, decided that he wanted to come and live with our family. After a week we headed to Houston.

Once in Houston, we settled in another apartment. My

parents enrolled me in second grade at a Catholic school. Catholic school was stricter than the public schools of Willcox and Portland. I didn't conform at first, but after making some adjustments, I excelled in my studies and was on track to complete second grade.

I wasn't too fond of Houston, especially with its insect problem. It was there that I was introduced to wasps. One afternoon, I was playing hide-and-seek outside with some of the other kids at the apartment complex. Not wanting to get caught, I ran behind this decent-size bush. I knew that there would be no way they would find me. All of a sudden, I hear this buzzing. Sure enough, it was a wasp nest. Before I could hightail it out of there, I was stung by two wasps. One nailed me on the right side of my face and the other on the left. Another time, I was climbing out of a window and accidentally stepped on a wasp nest. They stung me all over my legs.

I was relieved when Dad got tired of the wrestling business and the Houston territory. He quit the region and moved the family back to Willcox to live with my grandparents.

With Phoenix and Tucson a short driving distance from Willcox, Dad decided that he was going to start his own wrestling promotion in the state of Arizona. The promotion got off to a good start, but for whatever reason it just didn't work out.

While we were in Willcox, Dad convinced my grandma to sell pizza at the café. He knew there was profit in pizza. He taught my grandma how to make Italian pizza—the sauce, the dough, everything. I think my dad's dream was to have his own pizza restaurant after his wrestling career was over.

Grandma liked the idea and I even remember them installing this giant pizza oven. The Truck Stop Café was now selling pizza and it was a big hit.

Now in high school, Mike started playing football. He wanted to get better and stronger, and I remember Dad buying a weight set and helping Mike get in shape. He would set up the weights in the backyard, and that's where they would work out.

MIKE DIBIASE (brother):

Dad married Mom when I was about fourteen years old. I have always considered Mike DiBiase to be my father. He taught me a lot about life and especially sports. Since he was very athletic and sports-minded, we would spend hours and days together to help me become a great football player.

Word spread throughout town that my dad was training Mike. As a former football star, my dad was in excellent shape. The next thing we knew, there were kids coming from all over town wanting to work out and train.

I loved football. I really liked going to Mike's high school games to watch him play. I also used to accompany him to his practices and I would run up and down the sidelines, cheering him on. Although I was eight years old, I wanted to spend all my time with my older brother. He was the star tight end on the football team and I wanted to be just like him.

That Christmas, I was so happy when my parents got me a complete football uniform. It didn't take me long to decide that I wanted to be a professional football player. My brother Mike was a great influence on me.

MIKE DIBIASE:

I am eight years older than Ted. As the middle brother, he was always trying to hang around with me and my friends. I used to tease him and do other things older brothers are supposed to do. One time, I almost scared him to death.

Teddy and I always used to watch scary movies at Grandma's house on Saturday night on a program called *Saturday Night Chiller.* It was hosted by this sexy, female vampire-type character called Ghoulia. One night, I decided to scare Teddy. After the double feature, I told him to head home and that I would meet him there shortly. Our house was only two down. You couldn't turn the lights on because you didn't want to wake anyone. I gave him some time to get in bed. I was sure Teddy was waiting to hear the sound of the back door, but I made sure he didn't. I sneaked into the house and heard a frightened voice asking, "Mike, is that you?" I purposely didn't answer. As I walked throughout the house, the boards were creaking and I was making subtle noises. Ted asked again, "Come on, Mike, I know it's you!" I didn't respond. I sneaked closer and closer to Ted's bed. Just as he started to fade into the night, I leapt from the darkness and landed on top of Ted in his bed. I scared the you-know-what out of him. In fact, Teddy was so petrified, he not only started screaming at the top of his lungs, he also wet his pants!

With the failure of Dad's promotion, but with professional wrestling still in his blood, we once again packed up our bags and headed to another wrestling territory. This time we moved to Dad's hometown of Omaha. We settled in the same house that Dad had lived in with his first wife on South Twenty-second Street.

After working a few months in the territory, he once again quit wrestling. Tired of the politics, as well as promoters not properly paying off, he temporarily got out of the business. I recall Dad coming home one night and throwing his bag in the basement as if he would never grab it again.

Dad was my hero and I wanted to be just like him. He was bigger than life. He had a storied career at the University of Nebraska and I hoped to follow in his footsteps.

But Dad never wanted any of his kids to get involved with professional wrestling. Back then, wrestling was not a job that would make you rich. There were no benefits, health insurance, pension plan, or 401(k). If you were good, you could make a living. And if you were lucky, you could make a good living. As an adult, I now understand. I understand the hardships, the time away from one's family, and the insecurity.

OSCAR NANFITO (childhood friend):

The one thing that I always respected about Ted was his ambition. As early as ninth grade, he had direction and a vision. He wanted to make something of his life. He always wanted to be a professional wrestler and to be like his dad. I thought it was phony. But if that was what Ted really wanted to do for a living, then I supported it. Unlike me, at least Ted had a goal in life.

Dad had many connections through friends and family, and throughout our two years in Omaha, he tried a few other jobs. For a period of time he sold life insurance. He also hooked up with Mickey Sporano, a childhood friend. Mickey was in the nightclub business and hired my dad to manage a club. Neither venture provided any long-term success, and he eventually went back into the wrestling business.

Before we moved there, I had visited Omaha. For the first time, I was introduced to all my relatives on the DiBiase side. I remember Grandma Di-Biase, Aunt Betty, Aunt Mary, and many of my cousins. They were all super nice and showed me a tremendous amount of love. From the way they talked to the smell of the kitchen, you could tell the DiBiase family was real Italian.

We moved to the neighborhood where my dad grew up. The kids that I would meet and play with were the children of people that my dad had gone to school with when he was young. This was where I started to learn about the Italian culture.

Almost every Sunday we would have a huge lunch. All the relatives would gather at Grandma DiBiase's house. There would be an adult table and a kids' table. Before lunch, the men would be outside talking while the women were in the kitchen preparing the meal. The kids would play outside or huddle around the kitchen, trying to sneak a meatball.

I had already fallen in love with lasagna and spaghetti, and Sunday at Grandma's house was a feast. Besides the pasta and fresh Italian bread, there was always a meat, some vegetable, like eggplant, and pieces of salami, prosciutto, and cheese. And there was never a shortage of wine on the table. We would eat until the notches on our belt buckles were about to rip.

After the meal, the women would clear the table and the men would go back to the football game, business discussion, or whatever else they were doing. Some would even take a nap. The kids would go back outside to play.

About two hours or so later, Grandma or one of my aunts would gather everyone back to the table for dessert. You knew it was time for the sweets because of the aroma of freshly brewed coffee.

The desserts were out of this world. There would always be Italian cookies and pastries, such as almond macaroon tarts, sfogliatelles, pasticciotti, and éclairs. I would always grab a cannoli or two.

JOHN DIBIASE:

One Sunday afternoon, some of the relatives came over to our house for dinner. Mom was making lasagna, among other things, as the main course. Ted and I were sitting at the kids' table in the living room. As the food was coming out, Ted and I started fighting over something. He made me very mad. We started bickering back and forth until Ted got up to go do something—probably to check on the desserts. Seizing the opportunity, I spit in his lasagna! Ted came back and sat down to finish his food. He ate all the lasagna.

When he completed his meal, I looked at him and said, "How was your lasagna?"

"It was great."

"Good, because I spit in it!" I got in big trouble with my dad.

My neighborhood in Omaha was very ethnically diverse. You had the Italians to the east, the Poles to the west, the Germans to the north, and a few other groups scattered to the south. All the people who lived within eight to ten city blocks of my house were Italians.

The house we lived in on South Twenty-second Street was a small one-bedroom with a front porch. When you entered the house through the porch, there was a living room. To the left was the bedroom, with the only bathroom in the house. At the far end of the living room to the left was the kitchen. Just outside the kitchen, there were stairs that went down to the basement, which was unfinished and used for storage.

MIKE DiBIASE:

We had a Ping-Pong table in the basement. My cousins Johnny and Jim Sanchez and I used to play all the time. We were all six to eight years older than Teddy. Well, Teddy would always want to play and we wouldn't let him. Dad finally stepped in and said we had to let him play. So we did. At first we would just beat him real good until he would quit. But you know what? After a while, he started getting better and better. Pretty soon he was beating everyone. I was real proud of him.

There was also an upstairs attic, with a low ceiling that ran the entire length of the house. Dad remodeled it into a bedroom, and that's where Mike, John, and I slept. On one side, John and I shared a double bed and dresser; on the other, Mike had a twin bed and dresser.

There was no central air, just a window unit. During hot summer days, we spent as little time as possible in the attic. But sooner or later we had to sleep. So to keep it as cool as possible, we rigged two box fans in the upstairs windows to circulate the air and keep it cool.

The house was small, but it was ours. Outside of Grandma's house in Willcox, I had lived my entire life in an apartment. So I had nothing to complain about, and actually found the house quite satisfying.

We lived there for two years. I completed the fourth and fifth grades at St. Ann's Catholic School. I attended mass on a regular basis. I was very serious about my faith and took an interest in God at an early age. I even became an altar boy.

OSCAR NANFITO:

Ted was very committed and regularly attended church. We used to hang out in his room, and I would watch and listen to Ted studying the Latin responses to the prayers that were required of an altar boy.

I believe that even at an early age, Ted wanted to know about God. I always believed that Ted was searching for God. He always believed that there was something bigger than him.

I was very dedicated to my religious responsibility and never missed a mass. Whether there was a rain- or snowstorm, I was always there for the priest, and I was often recognized for my dedication.

St. Ann's was only one block from our house and across from the church was Columbus Park. I loved playing in that park. But I also got into some fights there.

As the son of a neighborhood legend and professional wrestler, I often was subjected to generous compliments, as well as immature harassment. It was only a matter of time before I would have to prove myself. Tim Lalley, a classmate, would be the person to drop the gauntlet.

Tim challenged me to a fight. I didn't have a beef with the kid, but he called me out. Word spread like wildfire, and the park across the street was soon sold out for the afternoon rumble between two fifth graders.

Tim apparently had some boxing training. When the bell rang, he came out boxing. The first thing I did when he threw a right jab was hook his arm. He immediately threw a left, and I also hooked that arm. I now had both of his arms under mine. I picked him up and took him to the ground and flat on his back. I was sitting on top of him, holding both of his arms to the ground. He was pinned and had nowhere to go.

As I reached back to punch him in the face, Tim pleaded, "Let me up. It isn't fair. We are supposed to be boxing. Let's box."

"No," I said. "Do you want to fight or not? There are no rules in a fight. I am either going to punch you in the face and knock your head off, or you are going to give up and we are going to walk away." It was good news for Tim that he chose the latter.

JOHN DiBIASE:

In the winter months, the city used to purposely flood a part of Columbus Park. It would soon freeze over and the kids in the neighborhood would use it as a hockey rink. One time, Ted was playing goalie. During the course of the game, somebody slapped a shot. Ted stopped the shot, but the puck hit him right in the face. The impact broke his nose. I ran home to get some help and told Dad what happened.

As Dad and I hurried to the park, we noticed that the guys had tended to Ted and were carrying him back to the house. My dad said, "Hey, Teddy, are your legs okay?"

"Yes sir. They are okay."

"Well, then, put him down and let him walk."

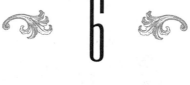

6

THE CHALLENGES OF BECOMING A MAN

Because of Mike's influence, I knew I wanted to play organized football. St. Ann's had a football team for its seventh and eighth graders. Although I was only in fourth grade, I was a big kid, so they let me try out. I was determined to make the team. And I did, as an offensive and defensive lineman.

In an unprecedented turn of events, I had earned a starting position as a fourth grader. My parents were so excited and proud. The

Playing high school football.

football field was directly across from my house, and my parents were there to support me at the first game of the season.

We were getting beat pretty bad. During halftime my father came up to me, and in front of my teammates he looked at me and said, "Are you afraid to hit that guy in front of you?"

"No, sir."

"Well, it sure looks like you are!"

My teammates thought the comments were unnecessary and some even called him a hard-ass. But I knew my dad; he wasn't chewing me out, but rather challenging me. He was just waiting for me to get aggressive on the field. When the final seconds on the clock ticked off, we got thumped and lost the game.

We walked back to the house in silence. Before I could even get changed out of my uniform, Dad grabbed a football and motioned me to the backyard. He said, "Let's go, Teddy. I want to teach you something."

The first thing he did was adjust my stance. Then he put the ball down in a hike position. "Okay, Teddy, as soon as I move the ball I want you to hit me as hard as you can." I was confused and didn't want to hit my dad. "Don't worry, you aren't going to hurt me. Just fire out and hit me as hard as you can when I move the ball."

When Dad moved the ball and I came off, he smacked me so hard that the impact knocked me over backward. Even though I was fully padded, it still hurt. He told me to come back and we did it again. Once again, he knocked me silly. We repeated it a few more times. After getting whacked four consecutive times, he had my attention. I was all fired up and he was really pissing me off.

I got back in my stance and started panting and snarling. I was mad and it was go time. Well, he moved that ball and I came out of stance and hit him with everything I had. Simultaneously, Dad grabbed me by my jersey and pulled me right into his face. "You are mad at me right now, aren't you?" I was still snarling, and at that point I didn't care that he was my father. "I bet you would like to kill me right now, wouldn't you?"

"Yes sir."

"Good! That is the kind of emotion that I want to see you play the game with every snap. Each time you get down in a stance, you need to think and feel the way you do right now. Don't ever forget it!" And I never did.

MIKE DIBIASE:

Even at an early age, Teddy was a very good football player. At ten years old, he placed nationally in the NFL's Punt, Pass & Kick competition.

Dad was desperately trying to get out of the wrestling business, but it seemed like he always managed to find his way back. After spending two years in Omaha, the summer before the start of sixth grade, we moved back to Amarillo.

The Amarillo territory was Dory Funk Sr.'s promotion. Dory and my dad were not only good friends, they always had classic wrestling battles. Dad was guaranteed he'd make a decent living and be able to provide for his family. The Funk family was always good to my father, and they treated our entire family with class and respect.

We moved into a decent apartment complex. I really liked the huge swimming pool, and we used it a lot that hot summer. Other wrestlers lived in the complex and they helped us settle in. One wrestler who I thought was pretty tough was "Killer" Karl Kox. Another worker who lived there and was kind and gracious to our family was Tim Woods. Tim and his wife, Tiger, were super folks and we really enjoyed their company.

Dad was a huge heel in Amarillo but he still managed to capture many titles in the territory. He was a one-time NWA International Tag Team Champion, with Danny Plechas, as well as a three-time NWA North American Tag Team Champion with Danny Plechas, Dr. X, and the legendary Fritz Von Erich, respectively. He was equally successful as a singles wrestler, winning the NWA North American Heavyweight Championship on three separate occasions.

I loved professional wrestling and especially watching my dad wrestle. Because he was a heel, I didn't go to a lot of the matches. Even when Dad would take me and my brothers, we would always have to be on alert. He made sure we always sat close to the dressing room. He reminded us, "If anything happens, if anyone comes up to you and starts trouble, or even if you feel scared, just walk right there into the dressing room. It will be okay."

There was one night at the Amarillo Sports Arena when things were getting out of hand. All of a sudden, Pampero Firpo came out of the dressing room and brought my brother John and me back in there. He said, "Stay here and don't move." They were obviously having a small riot. I then watched him put on these two black gloves and head out to the fight.

Unlike today—when you have families from many socioeconomic groups attending wrestling events—back then the wrestling crowd was pretty much blue-collar, and they were a rough bunch. I watched wrestling on TV every week; live events weren't for kids, especially not the children of heels.

I completed the sixth grade in Amarillo. I enjoyed school and made lots of new friends. I was still husky but starting to get taller. I had a crush on one girl, but I basically never had a girlfriend until high school.

During this time, I got my first BB gun. I was issued the gun under the condition that I would be extremely careful and shoot targets only under the eye of an adult. Well, I would often take off by myself, with the gun, and head to the pond at the apartment complex and shoot at the ducks. I don't think I ever hit one.

One day I was shooting my gun at a horse trailer behind our apartment. I was popping the trailer and the *ping* noise it made on contact was pretty cool. After I reloaded and fully cocked the gun, I pulled the trigger. Almost simultaneously, my little brother John emerged from behind the trailer. He stepped right in front of my aim, and *bang*, I accidentally shot him right in the chest. I quickly ran over to him. The BB didn't even break the skin, but he started crying and screaming. I tried to plead with him to calm down, but he ran inside to tell Dad.

Dad came outside and called for me to come. He snatched the BB gun from my hand and threw it in the closet, almost breaking it. I was so scared. Dad sat me down and began to chew me out. "What did I tell you? What would have happened if you hit him in his eye? You could have seriously hurt John!" I was crying and very upset. But I knew Dad was right and I told him so. Fortunately for me, this time, I was spared a serious spanking.

I remember my dad waking me up one time in the middle of the night. It was obvious that he had driven all night to get home, because he was still in his wrestling clothes. "Teddy, go wash your face. When you get done, immediately come down. I have to tell you something." I was still half asleep, but I washed my face and proceeded downstairs. When I got there he sat me down and said, "Your mother is leaving." I couldn't believe it.

What apparently happened was that after a show, my dad went to a hotel room where the boys were playing cards. They were drinking and having a grand old time. Meanwhile, all night long and into the morning, my mother was calling Dad's room, but there was no answer. My mom knew about life on the road, and she knew about the reputations of some of the other guys who fooled around with women. Although my dad never had that reputation, it was only human nature for my mom to think the worst. I guess it was guilt by association.

My heart sank. I ran outside and went around to the back of the apartment. I went inside the horse trailer—the one John had stepped out from behind when I shot him with my BB gun—and cried my eyes out. I started to pray and asked God to make things right. I told him that I loved my mom, and I loved my dad, and I wanted everything to work out. I didn't want to have to choose between my parents.

By the time I got back to the apartment, everything had calmed down. Mom was in the kitchen making breakfast. It seemed that everything was fine. Whatever my dad had to do to prove that he was where he was supposed to be the night before, fortunately for me, she believed him.

Later that summer, my dad had a match with Dory Funk Sr. at the Amarillo Sports Arena. It wasn't an ordinary match. It was a Texas Death match. In that match, pinfalls don't count. The only way you win a Texas Death match is when somebody isn't able to answer the bell.

In a record that to my knowledge still stands to this day, my dad and Dory Funk Sr.'s match went on for an unprecedented three and a half hours. To keep the crowd engaged for that long is a testament to their working abilities. If you think about it, a football game is more or less a three-hour event with a halftime, time-outs, and other short breaks.

During the course of this match, I heard on the radio that my dad and Dory were entering the second hour of their match. My mother worked it even for us. She reacted like she was all upset and told us not to go anywhere. She was going down to the sports arena.

It turned out that my mother was in on the match. To help build heat, Dory wanted my mother to speed through town and get stopped by the police. She got in her car and drove right through the heart of Amarillo, speeding and running every red light. She was trying to get stopped by the police, but nobody stopped her. She finally got to the arena and security detained her. My mom, who worked in the business for years, didn't miss a step with her performance to make it look real.

With my dad and Dory both tired and busted up, the finish of the match was even more astonishing. They knew that the city had a curfew. They had started their match around ten o'clock at night, and at that time it was already fifteen minutes past the one o'clock curfew. It was obvious that they were in direct violation of the city ordinance. The police and fire marshal were called in to shut the building down. They stopped the match and sent everyone home. In the end, Dad and Dory had wrestled a three-and-a-half-hour draw.

The next day it was all in the news. It was incredible. The arena was completely sold out for weeks.

We stayed only one year in Amarillo. Dad's run was over, and to avoid overexposure, it was time to move on. He made a decision, and it was crystal-clear that we were going back to Omaha to stay. However, Dad was still involved with wrestling. He would use Omaha as a base and drive to all the different wrestling regions. He wasn't moving anymore. At that time, Dad was wrestling for the Dusek family in the Nebraska territory.

Since kindergarten, I had moved eight times in seven years. But that was the nature of professional wrestling. Nobody ever complained, and we were a family that looked out for one another.

We even moved back into the same house we were living in before. I was enrolled again in St. Ann's Catholic School. There I spent seventh, eighth, and ninth grade. It was my longest tenure so far in one place. It was there that I met my friend of now over forty years, Oscar Nanfito.

Oscar and I became best friends. During those years, we were nearly inseparable. We played football and other sports, hung out, talked, and did other things young boys do in their early teens. My parents liked Oscar. We had chemistry and always got along great.

We were opposite in some areas, especially girls. Unlike me, Oscar would get all the girls. He was handsome and very confident. He had very little fear of women, or at least he played it that way.

One time, Oscar tried to help me. During our freshman year, Oscar's older brother Joe was getting married. At the wedding reception, there was this girl I really liked, but I didn't have the confidence to talk to her. Oscar used his charm and brought us together. We hung out and chatted for a while.

I told Oscar I really wanted to give her a kiss, but I was scared. He motivated me to make my move, and I did. Thanks, Oscar!

OSCAR NANFITO:

Ted liked her and she liked Ted. So I got both of them together. Ted wanted to give her a kiss but he was scared. I said, "Oh, just kiss her! Go outside and give her a kiss. Don't worry about it!" Well, he did, but the fun was just starting. To my surprise, I noticed Ted was eyeing another girl. I couldn't believe it. The next thing I saw, they were talking. We somehow got separated and I couldn't find Ted. I finally decided to look outside. Lo and behold, I see Ted and this girl on the swing, smooching away. I told him later that I thought I created a monster!

The summer prior to my freshman year in high school, my life changed. St. Ann's only went up to the eighth grade. I wanted to attend and play football at Creighton Preparatory School, a private, Jesuit college prep school for young men that was founded in 1878.

It was a very competitive school. You had to take and pass an entrance exam to get accepted. The school had a marvelous academic reputation, and its athletics were equally impressive. Though I was just an average student, I passed the exam and was accepted into the school.

OSCAR NANFITO:

Ted was a really good student. He would take honors classes, study real hard, and get As and Bs all the time. I was just the opposite. I was a D/F, barely pass type of guy. Unlike Ted, I was just a goof-off.

It was then that I asked my dad to help me get in shape. I really wanted to be a standout football player, just like him. I also wanted to make him proud. It was time to get serious. Dad said, "If you want to play football because you really want to, that's fine. But if you're doing this because you think you have to because I did, don't do it."

"Dad, I understand what you are saying, but I am doing this because I want to."

"Teddy, I will help you. I'll also work you hard."

"I want it, sir."

Then he looked me straight in the eye. "Teddy, I love you no matter what. Be the best you can be at whatever it is you do. But remember, what I am about to put you through to get you in shape, you asked for it!"

Boy, did he give it to me. For the next four months and throughout my freshman year, Dad trained me. He worked me very hard and taught me the importance of weights, cardiovascular training, and eating right. I worked muscles that I didn't even know I had. Though I would get sore, I never got depressed or upset. I was focused; I had my eye on that football prize.

I also recruited my buddy Oscar to work out with me. He was also a football player and wanted to get in better shape for the upcoming season. Dad's training schedule had us first doing calisthenics. And we did them until we dropped. We then ran, anywhere from five to ten miles a day. But it wasn't over yet. We would then stumble into our garage for a detailed weight work-out—bench-pressing, squats, dead-lifts, and so on. After months of this work-out, we were in excellent shape and had become football machines.

OSCAR NANFITO:

Ted's dad helped both of us get in shape for football season. Mr. DiBiase was a disciplinarian. He was strict and didn't pull any punches. When he wanted something, he told you exactly what he wanted. He was big and burly and he had this deep, scary voice. I was always intimidated by him. Even when he was laughing, you would have to wonder. Don't get me wrong, he was a nice guy. But if he said something, you knew you'd better do it.

After my freshman year at Creighton Prep, we moved back to Amarillo. Dad decided that because of my football potential, it would be better for me to attend a high school in Texas. There, the high school football talent was much better. The competition would give me an opportunity to improve and hopefully get a college scholarship. It was also an opportunity for Dad to finish out his wrestling career.

The Amarillo territory was a great place to make a living wrestling. The promoter was Dory Funk. Unlike in past moves, this time we took everything with us back to Amarillo. Dad made it unequivocally clear that he wasn't moving the family again until I graduated high school.

Since I had three years of high school left, Dad only wanted to wrestle up until I graduated from high school. He would then retire from the sport and relocate the family back to Willcox. There he would begin his second career, running his own pizza restaurant.

We arrived in May and settled into an apartment. It was the same complex that we lived in years ago. Mom wasn't too impressed with the property this time around and wanted a more desirable place to live. We eventually moved into another apartment complex at the end of June. We planned on staying there for the next three years.

It now seemed that our life was finally stable. I was working out harder than ever before. My parents were getting along very well. John was enjoying his new friends. Now that the DiBiase family was all together, we were living *la dolce vita*—the sweet life. Then everything went downhill.

Wednesday, July 2, 1969, was the worst day of my life. My best friend, my dad, Mike DiBiase, died. Dad was wrestling Man Mountain Mike in Lubbock. Mike was a big man, about six-four, and weighed more than four hundred pounds. During the course of the match, Mike threw Dad out of the ring. As Dad proceeded to get back in the ring by grabbing the second rope, he collapsed and fell facedown on the floor.

The fans thought nothing was out of the ordinary and the referee began his count. As the referee was counting, things weren't going as planned. Harley Race, a wrestler who would later become one of the greatest in the history of the sport, was standing in the back, watching the match. He sensed something was wrong and rushed to the ring. He performed CPR and did the best to breathe life into my dad. An ambulance was called and Dad, with Harley by his side, was rushed to the hospital. He was pronounced dead on the emergency room table.

HARLEY RACE:

Earlier in the evening, Mike DiBiase told me that he moved all his belongings and his entire family from one apartment to another that same day. He looked very tired, but didn't complain about a thing. I think half of the reason he didn't complain was because he was wrestling Man Mountain Mike. MMM weighed more than four hundred pounds, so Mike knew he wasn't going to be moving at any high speed.

As the match started, there was some pushing and shoving. Mike then took a back bump. All of a sudden, Mike folded his arms over his chest, backed up into the ropes, and went right out onto the floor.

I was watching the match from the back and immediately knew something was wrong. I ran to ringside and tended to Mike. He had a pulse but wasn't breathing. I administered CPR and did my best to keep him alive until the ambulance arrived. He was alive when they left in the ambulance.

TERRY FUNK:

A lot of people don't know this, but I didn't go to Lubbock the night Teddy's father died. In fact, that was the reason why Mike went. Teddy's father took my place that night to wrestle Man Mountain Mike. He was very tired, but being the person that he was, he took my place anyway. I wish I would have gone.

At the news of Dad's death, I immediately started to cry. I was dazed and in disbelief. Mom went hysterical. I never saw her in such distress. She was out of control and I remember her screaming at the top of her lungs, "This can't be true!"

Though he didn't actually know what was wrong, John was equally shaken by the events. With Mom unable to gather her faculties, I had to tell John. I remembered what Dad had told me when his mother passed away. I told my concerned brother, "John, Dad died tonight." We cried and embraced each other as tight as we could. Suddenly, in a divine moment, John pulled back and said to me exactly what Dad told us after his mother died: "Teddy, Dad's at peace. He's looking down on us right now. He's fine." It was the worst night of my life.

JOHN DiBIASE:

The night my father died, they came to the door, and Teddy answered. They asked for Mom. She started crying. I knew something was wrong. Then they spoke to Teddy. Then I was told—I was the last one to know. But I sensed something was wrong, and if I remember it right, Teddy may have been the one to tell me that Dad had died. I was only eight years old.

That Saturday, July 5, the funeral services were held in Amarillo. The local funeral home was packed with family and friends. My brother Michael got leave from the army and was there with his wife. My dad had touched so many people, and I was shaken by seeing him in a casket. I had to be pulled away when they closed the lid. Dad's body was later shipped to Willcox, where he was buried.

Under Texas law, an autopsy is required. It was discovered that Dad had a heart attack. He had arterial sclerosis—a hardening or thickening of the walls of the arteries—and one artery was completely blocked. Scar tissue was found around his heart, showing he had had earlier heart attacks.

With Dad's untimely death, Mom had no choice but to move the family back to Willcox. Our budget was limited. Some of Dad's wrestling friends and family helped us out as best they could, as there was no way we could live on our own. So, with the help of some family and friends, we packed all our belongings and headed back to Grandma's house.

The next few months after Dad's death were a time of grief for me and my family. My mother, who had been drinking prior to Dad's death, had now become dependent on alcohol. She was devastated and wouldn't even leave the house. She didn't have a job, so she had nothing but time on her hands.

It was getting out of control. All she would do was lie around the house, drinking and smoking. Eventually, she developed emphysema and had to have her gall bladder removed. At the time, my grandmother had to raise John and me, and was doing all she could to pull my mother out of her depression. But nothing seemed to work.

One day, out of desperation, my grandmother made a phone call to the one and only person she thought could help: my biological father, Ted Wills. "Ted, Helen is in really bad shape. Nothing seems to help. I think you should come out here and visit with her. Maybe if she saw you, she might feel better."

"Is that a good idea? Are you sure she wants to see me?"

Grandma added, "Ted, your son needs a dad." She was worried about me.

A few weeks later, Ted returned to Willcox. His goal was to help lift my mother from her depression and reestablish a relationship with me. He accomplished the former but failed at the latter. Besides some sporadic weekend visits, cards, and a present every birthday and Christmas, I had very little interaction with Ted.

As for my mother, she was flattered that Ted had come back to help her, and she responded well to him. We were all happy when Mom would go out to eat with Ted or go for a walk. He was the best medicine for her. She was very lonely and she needed companionship and someone to take care of her. I think Ted came back because he always cared about me and my mom. A few months later, Ted and Mom remarried.

As for Ted and me, I must say, I was curious to see him again. We were very cordial to each other. I was very happy that he had expressed such concern for Mom. Here's the thing: as I got to know him, I thought he was a good man and a nice guy. But I really didn't consider him my father. Mike DiBiase was my father, and nobody could ever take Mike's place.

After Mom and Ted remarried, they moved to Ted's place in Los Angeles with John. Ted had a good job with the television networks as a lighting technician. He worked the lighting on games and entertainment shows such as *The Dating Game* and *The Newlywed Game, General Hospital,* and *American Bandstand.* He made a very good living.

I guess they had expected that I would go with them, but I refused. The thought of living in Los Angeles didn't appeal to me at all. I just wanted to stay with my grandparents in Willcox. I was focused on working out and football. I really missed my mom and especially John. The irony of it was that John was headed off to be raised by my biological father, while I had just spent the last ten years being raised by his biological father.

Because of Grandma's help, I was able to attend the tenth grade at Willcox High School. If there was a place where I could regain my focus, it was on the football field. During every practice, I thought about my dad and remembered everything he had taught me. I channeled all my sadness into making him proud of me via football.

I was physically ready because of the time Dad had spent with me training the summer before. I was fifteen years old, stood six feet two inches tall, and weighed two hundred pounds. I was determined to be a success on the gridiron. I wasn't about to let him down. And I didn't. As a sophomore, I made the varsity football team, starting both as an offensive tackle and defensive tackle for the Willcox High Cowboys.

At the first game of the season, with tears running down my face, I spoke to my dad during the singing of the national anthem. "Dad, this game is for you. I know you are not physically here, but I know you're watching." That day, I had my greatest individual performance ever in a football game: twelve unassisted tackles, a blocked punt, and a knocked-down pass—and I recovered a fumble for our victory. I didn't let Dad down and I knew he was proud of me.

For the rest of the season, I excelled on the football field and in every game. Besides my studies and working at my grandmother's café, football was all I lived for. I never lost sight of what Dad had taught me. My success produced both accolades and jealousy. I went out on the field to be the best player I could and to help our team win. I was named to the All-Conference First Team, as well as an All-State Honorable Mention. However, we ended the season with a disappointing 3–7 record.

After the season ended, I became even more focused. I wanted to be better and worked out harder to attain a college football scholarship. I hit the weights and kept running. I joined the track-and-field team so I could throw the shot put in order to stay in shape. By then it had become common knowledge that I wanted to be the first student from Willcox High School to be offered a full football scholarship at an NCAA Division I university.

At the end of the school semester, when we recessed for Christmas, my focus was broken: in December of 1969, I met my first love. Dixie Lee Stow was the most beautiful girl I had ever seen. I met her while she was visiting family in Willcox. She lived in Casa Grande, Arizona, about 150 miles away. We spent the entire Christmas vacation together. Eventually she had to go home, but we were both madly in love with each other. Her parents were super nice and they treated me like family.

Dixie and I were both the same age, and not yet old enough to drive. So for the remainder of my sophomore year, we would talk on the phone every day for hours. During the various school breaks throughout the year, either I would go to her house or she would come to Willcox. If I wasn't working out or in the café, I was with Dixie.

Then, the summer before my junior year, I decided to take a part-time job as a lifeguard at the city pool. In between working at the café, workouts, and lifeguarding, the rest of my time was with and about Dixie. We were inseparable. Because of the relationship, my focus on football was negatively affected.

Not only was I madly in love, I could also talk to Dixie. Since the death of my father, I really hadn't had a person I could talk to like I could with him. We dated for a year and a half. Our long-distance relationship came to an end in the late summer prior to my senior year.

7

THE FINAL TWO YEARS OF HIGH SCHOOL

My junior year of high school was a dichotomy. I was in love with Dixie but also committed to playing football at a high level. My problem was that I wasn't accomplishing the latter. Dad had told me not to get serious about girls in high school: "Girls and athletics don't mix." With Dad gone, my mother drinking, and Mike in the military, I was looking for affection. I yearned for someone. Dixie filled that void.

MIKE DIBIASE:

I couldn't believe that Ted was losing his focus. I was concerned
about him blowing everything he had worked so hard for because of
this girl. He would spend every available moment talking to, thinking
about, and visiting with her. When he got his license, he took
Grandma's car and drove almost every weekend to see Dixie some
150 miles away. What was even more unreal was that back in 1970,
Ted was running up a phone bill in the neighborhood of three to four
hundred dollars a month! I jumped all over Ted and tried to get him
to stay focused. I even went as far as asking him what he would do if
Dixie got pregnant. Ted basically said he had everything under
control.

Ted also met my former army friend Robert "Abe" Lincoln.
Abe befriended Ted and they took a liking to each other. Abe told Ted
the same things I had stressed, but I guess since Abe wasn't his
brother and his approach was slightly gentler, Ted opened up. Abe
genuinely cared for Ted and got him to release lots of emotion. In the
end, Abe told him to stay focused on football. It was time for him to
get his mind off Dixie and back on football. Ted eventually broke up
with Dixie prior to his senior year.

With Dixie on my mind and in my heart, my junior football season was
mediocre. As a team, we did much better than the year before. We went 7–3.
It was a relief to have a winning season. I played decent enough to have some
standout games. I even received All-Conference honors. But it wasn't the level
of football that I should have been playing at.

At Creighton Prep, we were a football powerhouse and one of the best
schools in the state of Nebraska. It was a school steeped in tradition, and only
the crème de la crème were recruited to attend. Every player's goal was to
earn a scholarship at a major NCAA Division I school. At Willcox High, all the
players wanted to do was to get a letter.

During my junior year, my grandfather died. He passed away around

Thanksgiving. I loved him dearly; he never complained a day in his life about anything. But one day he said to me, "Teddy, I think I need to go see a doctor. I had a rough night." He was too old to drive, so I immediately drove him to the family physician. I waited anxiously while Grandpa was being examined. After about an hour, the doctor told me, "Ted, your grandpa has suffered a minor heart attack. He is still alive, but frankly, there is really nothing we can do for him right now. Take him home and watch him closely. If he has another bad night, bring him back in the morning."

Grandpa had another restless night. He called me into the room and said, "Teddy, I think you need to take me to the hospital." I freaked out. Grandpa got up, dressed on his own, and walked to the car.

He must have stayed in the hospital for about two weeks. Grandma stayed there with him. Every day after school I would visit him. I vividly remember seeing his feet—they were cold and purple. I asked the doctor what was wrong, and he told me that his blood wasn't properly circulating. Basically, he was wearing out. He was dying.

To make him more comfortable, I would rub his head and encourage him as much as possible. I would bring his electric razor to the room and shave him. I even tried joking with him a few days before Thanksgiving. I said, "Grandpa, you need to get out of this dang hospital bed. It's almost Turkey Day. There is going to be lots of food, and your favorite, pumpkin pie."

Grandpa looked at me and in a matter-of-fact way, which sent a chill down my spine, said, "Teddy, in a couple of more days I am going to be in the cemetery with your dad." Two days later Grandpa died. He was eighty-nine. It was a sad holiday season.

I put all my energy into football. That summer, I hit the weights, ran, and worked out hard. I was focused and reenergized. I had an outstanding summer practice and was fully prepared to have the season of my life. I was going to get a college football scholarship.

My determination to succeed and my skills on and off the field caused some jealousy among teammates and fellow classmates. As a lark, I was coerced by my friends to run for senior class president. After entering the race, I began to take it more seriously. With the jocks by my side, I was victorious.

I tried to be the leader on the team and I often challenged the other players. Mitch Plough and some of my other teammates apparently didn't like my aggressiveness. Now that the newcomer was a standout on the football field and the senior class president, rumors started circulating: apparently Mitch and some others were talking behind my back. One day, I walked right up to him and said, "Look, if you have a problem with me, here I am. If you have something to say to me, say it to my face, or just shut up." Mitch quickly backed down, and we would later become friends.

On the football field, my senior season was outstanding. Now at six-four and 225 pounds, I was blowing people off the line left and right, and was a terror on the defensive side of the ball. In the end, all my hard work paid off. I was personally recognized for my football accomplishments: First Team, All-Conference Offensive and Defensive Tackle; First Team, All-State Defensive Tackle; and the first Willcox football player invited to play in the All-State high school football game.

After football season, I focused on my studies and waited for track season to start so I could stay in shape. During Christmas break, I went to Los Angeles to spend the holidays with Ted, Mom, and John.

When classes started again in January, I was determined to work out harder than ever before. I believed that I had a good enough senior year in football to receive a college scholarship. And I was right.

One day, while I was in government class, trying to stay awake, I hid behind my friend Kathy Lindsey and tried to absorb the lecture. All of a sudden I heard over the loudspeaker, "Ted DiBiase, please report to the main office immediately." Kathy turned around in concern and said, "What did you do?" I didn't have a clue.

As I opened the door to the principal's office, he energetically said, "Ted, please come in. There are some people here who are really interested in talking to you." I introduced myself to three football coaches from the University of Arizona. After a few minutes of casual chit-chat, where they spoke highly of my football talents, one of the coaches said, "Ted, I have been sent here to ask you a question: Would you like to accept a full scholarship to play football at the University of Arizona?"

To say I was excited would be an understatement. I couldn't believe it. Without hesitation I accepted. I signed a conference letter of intent—meaning

I couldn't sign with any other team in the WAC (Western Athletic Conference). The press was there and the next day my picture was on the front page of the local paper.

As I left the principal's office and headed back to class, I was on cloud nine. I couldn't wait to tell all my family and friends. I thought it was poetic justice that the class I got called out of was a class of my immediate peers, some of whom doubted that I would accomplish my goal. When I got back to class, the teacher—who was also a football coach—asked, "So, what did you say?"

I passionately replied, "I'm going!"

Coach made the announcement to the entire class. "Class, Ted has just been offered a full scholarship to play football at the University of Arizona. This is a first in the history of Willcox High School. Let's all congratulate Ted." After a few moments of complete silence—you could have heard a pin drop— the class erupted into applause. Kathy and I hugged while others were giving me high fives.

After school, I rushed home and told my grandmother all about the football scholarship. I then called my mom and Ted right away. I said, "I'm going to the University of Arizona! I am going to be a Wildcat!" I also spoke to John, who was very excited for me. It seemed like I was on the telephone all night. My last call was to my ex-girlfriend, Dixie. It was a perfect ending to a perfect day.

A couple of weeks later, my friend Arthur and some others wanted to take me out to celebrate. Arthur said, "Hey, Ted, let's celebrate. You're Italian. All you Italians drink wine. Let's go have a glass of wine."

I cautiously said, "Okay." Keep in mind that up until the spring of my senior year in high school, I had never consumed intoxicating liquors. Not a glass of wine or even a bottle of beer.

That Saturday afternoon, Arthur picked me up in his car and we headed into town. He had this huge gallon of cheap Spanada red wine in the car. I think the entire gallon cost him only $1.98. He pulled into the local Dairy Queen, where he got two large plastic cups and packed them down with crushed ice. We then poured the wine over the ice. I started sipping it through a straw. Arthur and I finished off the entire gallon while cruising the town all afternoon and evening. I was drunk! That night, Arthur and some of my friends had to help me into Arthur's home, where I spent the night. The next morning I had the worst headache. It was my first hangover.

A couple of weeks later, I was at home relaxing, just watching TV. A commercial came on announcing that professional wrestling was coming to the Tucson Community Center. And it wasn't just any wrestling show. It was the wrestling show from the Amarillo territory. I couldn't believe it. It was the first time I had seen anything about professional wrestling in three years.

The commercial had all my old pals in it, including Dory Funk Sr. and Jr., Terry Funk, and Ricky Romero. I was so excited. I immediately said to myself that I was going to buy a ticket and go see them. I thought it would be very nice to see some of my old friends from Texas who I hadn't seen in years.

A few days later, I borrowed Grandma's Chevy Caprice and headed to Tucson. I got there early and patiently waited to see the boys. Finally, I saw one of the crew members and asked if any of the wrestlers were there yet. He directed me around the corner. Immediately, I saw Dory Funk Sr. and his son, Dory Jr. They looked at me and said, "Teddy, is that you?" We embraced. They were happy to see me and vice versa. I told them about my scholarship and they were so proud. It was like a family reunion.

We chatted for some time, but they had to get ready for the show. I asked about Terry Funk, who is the youngest of the Funk boys. Growing up, though he was eight years older than me, I was always the closest with Terry. Dory said, "Terry is not with us this trip. But we are coming back to Tucson in about a month. Terry will be with us then. I am sure he would love to see you." I stayed through the whole evening. What a great wrestling show.

The next time I returned to Tucson for the wrestling show, right away I inquired about Terry. When we saw each other, we embraced. I told him about everything I had accomplished and my plans to go to the University of Arizona. He was very proud of me. It was so good to see and talk with my friend. I felt so comfortable around Terry and all the other wrestlers. All of a sudden Terry said, "Teddy, why don't you come back to Amarillo and visit West Texas State? Take a recruiting trip. They will pay for it. Come to Amarillo and visit the school and at the same time you can see all of us. Who knows, you may even like the school."

TERRY FUNK:

Back then, West Texas State had a very good football program, a great coaching staff, and produced some great professionals like Mercury Morris and Duane Thomas. As a graduate of West Texas State, I told Teddy to give them a look.

It didn't take too much convincing, because he loved the area and also the many professional wrestlers they produced, such as Bruiser Brody, Stan Hansen, and me. Teddy was born into the business and always loved the sport. This was a key factor in Teddy choosing West Texas State over Arizona. Here he would have an opportunity to play college football and possibly get into the wrestling world.

West Texas State is where Terry as well as his brother, Dory Funk Jr., went to school. It has produced wrestlers such as Dusty Rhodes, Stan Hansen, Merced Solis (Tito Santana), Tully Blanchard, Barry Windham, Bruiser Brody, and Bobby Duncum.

I took my recruiting trip to Canyon to visit the campus and its facilities. In my mind, I was all set and ready to play for the University of Arizona. I didn't think anything about visiting my old stomping grounds on West Texas State's coin.

To my surprise, I really liked the campus. Everyone was very nice. The head football coach, Gene Mayfield, was very friendly. In fact, prior to coaching at West Texas State, Coach Mayfield built a high school football powerhouse at Permian in Odessa. It was the school program that inspired the 2004 movie *Friday Night Lights*.

Coach and his staff showed me lots of personal attention. I was offered a full scholarship to play football for the Buffaloes. Before I headed back home to Willcox, I accepted Coach's offer and signed a conference letter of intent. I thought West Texas State would be a great opportunity to improve my football skills so I could eventually play professionally. They were a Division I school and played in the Missouri Valley Conference.

I also thought that if for some reason I wasn't good enough to get drafted, and if I didn't make it in professional football, I would have more opportunities in Amarillo than in Tucson. What I was really thinking about was becoming a professional wrestler. My dad never wanted me to be a professional wrestler. Never. But deep down, I never could let go of my desire to one day become a wrestler just like Dad.

I headed back to Willcox quite confused. I told my grandma everything, and she told me to follow my heart. I did. I made up my mind that I was going to attend West Texas State University.

One day at school, I got called out of class to the principal's office. Upon my arrival, I was surprised to see three men again: the head football coach, the defensive line coach, and the amateur wrestling coach of the University of Arizona. They invited me to lunch to discuss my future at the University of Arizona. Word had apparently got out that I had visited and signed a letter of intent with West Texas State.

During lunch, we had a nice conversation. The coaches were puzzled because they thought I wanted to attend their school. I was honest with them and told them how I felt. I stressed that whether I attended the University of Arizona or West Texas State, there was no assurance I would be good enough to make it into the NFL—hence my other passion in life, becoming a professional wrestler. I think that's why they brought the school's amateur wrestling coach, who told me they would put me on the school's wrestling team. Obviously, they didn't understand a word I had said. I had no interest in amateur wrestling. In fact, I had my mind made up to sign with West Texas State. At that point, I was simply just trying to be nice.

As our lunch ended, they invited me to the upcoming athletic banquet on campus for incoming freshmen. The banquet was scheduled for the evening of National Signing Day. Coach said, "Ted, the least you can do for us is to come to the banquet. Just come, visit the campus, and see our facilities."

Beaten down, I said, "Okay. I will come to the banquet."

A couple of weeks later, the assistant football coach, who was a University of Arizona alumnus, drove me to the banquet. He was a great guy and I respected him a lot. During the two-and-a-half-hour drive, we chatted about lots of things. But he also warned me. He said, "Ted, I am going to be real honest with you because I like you. These guys are high pressure. You need to be prepared. They will be putting lots of pressure on you to sign a letter of intent. This is for sure. They are expecting me to tell you to attend the University of Arizona. But I am telling you that you need to do whatever you feel in your heart."

It was a great evening. The food was fantastic and the atmosphere was very regal. I met lots of guys from around the state and country, all of whom were going to attend the University of Arizona. Although I was enjoying the evening, with every passing minute my heart was leaning more and more to West Texas State. As I was getting ready to head back to Willcox, the coaches told me to spend the night in Tucson. They took care of all accommodations and put me up in a nice hotel.

The next morning I was awakened by a phone call around seven. It was the defensive line coach. He invited me down to join him and the other coaches for breakfast. I accepted, and met the coaches in the hotel restaurant. As I was eating, the coaches made one last effort to get me to commit. For some reason, I recall looking at the clock. It showed eight. Simultaneously, one of the coaches reached into his sport-coat pocket and pulled out a contract. He slid the contract to me from across the table and handed me a pen. "Ted, we want you to be the first person this year to sign the National Letter of Intent to play football for the University of Arizona."

I was flattered and appreciated the gesture. Though I was nervous, I stuck to my guns. "Coach, I still don't know." The coaches remained cordial, but they really wanted me to sign. I guess they were getting desperate, because they tried to play me for a fool. One of the coaches said, "Ted, go ahead, just sign it. If you change your mind, we will just tear it up."

I couldn't believe it. I may not have been the brightest guy, but I didn't just fall off a turnip truck either. I just sat there, and even though I wanted to say it out loud, I bit my tongue and simply thought, "You son of a bitch! Do you think I'm that stupid?"

But once again, I didn't budge. I stressed that I couldn't sign with them right now. They backed off. We ended breakfast shaking hands, and they told me one of the coaches would take me home. I went back to the room and packed my stuff. It was a long ride back to Willcox.

As soon as I got home, I couldn't wait to see my grandmother and tell her what had happened. I told her how everything was so intense and pressure-packed. She hugged me and told me how proud she was of the way that I handled myself. She also told me that Coach Dawson from West Texas State had been calling every fifteen minutes!

Coach Dawson, the running-back coach at West Texas State, was calling to get me to sign. My grandmother told him that I was at a banquet at the University of Arizona. They were obviously in a state of panic at West Texas State, because they thought I would be wooed into signing with the Wildcats.

I told Grandma of my plans and she agreed. I picked up the phone and called Coach Dawson, "Ted, we still want you. You didn't sign with Arizona, did you?"

"No sir. I didn't sign."

"I can be on a plane in ten minutes. I can come up right now and have you sign the letter of intent that makes it official."

"That won't be necessary, Coach Dawson. I'm not going to sign with any other school. Just put your letter in the mail. I'll sign it and return it right away."

I am pretty sure Coach Dawson still wasn't reassured. Not wanting to lose the deal, he probed, "Are you sure we don't need to fly over and bring the letter?"

I replied, "No, don't worry. I've given you my word. I am absolutely positive. The mail will be fine." And that was that. I made my decision to attend West Texas State University to play football and earn a degree in education.

With only a few months until graduation, I focused on my classes and working out. I partied with my friends and counted the days before I left for Amarillo. As the senior class president, I was required to give a graduation speech. I spoke to the class from my heart. I emphasized that you should always follow your dreams. That you can do whatever you want if you work hard at it. As long as you give 110 percent and do it to the best of your ability, then you will always be a success.

I couldn't wait to pack my bags and head to Amarillo, but I was really going to miss my grandma. A few weeks after graduation, as I was packing my stuff, Grandma entered my room. With tears in her eyes, she asked if I needed any help. We hugged and bawled for what seemed like hours. I can't even begin to explain how much my grandmother meant to me. I loved her so much and she was everything in my life. She was my refuge. I was going to miss her dearly.

8

WEST TEXAS STATE

My mom, Ted, and John all attended my high school graduation. Mike couldn't make it because he was still in the army. As we celebrated, Mom said she was going to be the one to drive me to college when I was ready to leave. Less than a month after graduation, I was ready to head out to Canyon. In the hot Willcox summer of 1972, I loaded Mom's car with my basics and her oxygen tank. Her emphysema was so bad that she needed the tank to breathe. After

hugging Grandma and finally letting go, Mom and I hit the road for the ten-hour drive to Texas.

It was my mom's first trip to Texas since my father died. Prior to heading to campus, we decided to spend a week or so with the Funks. I was especially happy for Mom. She and Dory Funk Sr.'s ex-wife, Dorothy, were real good friends. They hadn't seen each other in years. Mom stayed at her house. I was going to stay with Terry and his wife, Vicki. But when we arrived at Dorothy's house, Terry was also there. After I settled my mom in, Terry said,

"Teddy, pack your bags. You're coming with me. Along with Dick Murdoch, we are going on a four-day wrestling trip. It's your graduation gift." It was my first wrestling trip with the boys.

I had a great time. We visited Albuquerque, El Paso, and Odessa. Although I enjoyed the conversation, they were long trips: two hundred seventy miles from Amarillo to Albuquerque; two hundred seventy miles from Albuquerque to El Paso; two hundred eighty-five miles from El Paso to Odessa; and two hundred seventy miles from Odessa to Amarillo.

When we'd arrive at the venues, I would watch the matches. In Albuquerque, the first wrestler I saw was Harley Race. I never forgot Harley and how he had tried to save my dad's life. We spent some time together and reminisced. He was proud of my football accomplishments and knew that my dad had been proud of me as well. In fact, we are still good friends even to this day.

At the conclusion of each show, I would go out with the boys to eat and drink. With respect to drinking, I was making up for lost time. We would drink beer by the case. Terry treated me like a younger brother and during the entire trip, I never had to go into my pocket once. After partying all night, we would hit the sack and then get right back up and hit the road again.

When the trip was over, Terry dropped me off at his mother's house. I briefly visited with my mom and then went right to bed. The next morning I woke up with a terrible headache. I had the worst hangover. Unbeknownst to me, my mother had a cure. She cleaned her oxygen mask, put the mask on me, and told me to start breathing. I was skeptical at first, but after about ten minutes of breathing pure oxygen, my headache was gone.

The next morning, Mom told me she had a surprise: a graduation gift. After my father died, the federal government started sending my mother Social Security checks. Since I was living with my grandmother, for three years my mother had been giving her a monthly check to help with my expenses.

Well, Grandma didn't spend a single penny of that money. Mom handed me a lump-sum check, plus a little extra, for me to put down on a new car. I was ecstatic. Together we went down to the local Chevrolet dealer and I purchased my first car, a Chevy Nova. It was a two-door, blue sports car, with a white top and white bucket seats.

A few days later, we said our good-byes to the Funks in Amarillo. I hugged Mom and watched her leave for Los Angeles. I headed to Canyon. I had made arrangements to arrive at the campus early; they had no problem putting me up for the summer, and they even helped me obtain employment. Many players stayed on campus for the summer either to attend class or to work.

I stayed in Terrill Hall. At that time, it was the dorm for all the athletes. Any jock on a scholarship lived there—basketball, football, baseball, etc. The dorm was rectangular-shaped with a courtyard in the middle. There were eight rooms per unit. Each unit had its own living area with a community bathroom. Though there were usually two people per room, for the summer I had my own room. After that, my permanent roommate was Jeff Lloyd.

The cafeteria food was decent. I loved to eat and took advantage of the three meals a day. It wasn't Grandma's cooking, but I would always eat their hamburger steaks. They were so thick and hard and often referred to as hockey pucks. Although there was plenty of food, I often craved Mama DiBiase's lasagna.

My summer job was at the Randall County Feed Lot. I sincerely believe that they created this job just for me. The lot housed ninety thousand head of cattle. And yes, they left behind mountains upon mountains of droppings. There were literally hundreds of these fifteen-foot-high manure mounds throughout the feed lot.

In the middle of the lot, they had this big grain feeder. It was where the cows were fed. My minimum-wage job was to push a broom for twelve hours a day. I was required to keep the grain from overflowing on the roof so that it didn't collapse. It was a cake job, but it was boring.

After a few weeks, I hooked back up with the Funks. Every Thursday night I would go see their weekly show in Amarillo. Afterward, Terry and his wife, Vicki, would take me out drinking. One night I got so drunk. When I got up for work the next morning, my stomach was churning. Once I arrived at work, I started puking my guts out. I had one of my buddies tell the boss I was sick. The pattern continued for about a month until I couldn't take it anymore. I eventually stayed away from Amarillo on Thursday nights.

TERRY FUNK:

It was just part of the wrestling business. After the matches, you take your wife and friends out to eat and drink some beer. It was a pretty big deal for Teddy, because I was always paying for it. I wasn't buying him five-dollar whiskey shots, rather cheap beer. Still, Teddy thought I was a high roller. I never took him out during football season!

Because my job was so boring, I would often take a nap in a nearby cubby-hole. One time, one of the bosses caught me sleeping on the job. They called me into the office and I immediately apologized. "I'm sorry. I'm not lazy. Please don't fire me. I promise you it will never happen again." They didn't fire me. Rather, I was reassigned to work inside the grain pit. It would be hot as blazes, and my job was to make sure the pit didn't overflow or get clogged, so that the grain feeder would keep running properly. Wearing a mask, I had to stay inside the pit and shovel the grain away from the feeder's opening so the hole wouldn't clog.

After a few weeks, I asked Terry if he could help me find another job. I wasn't lazy or afraid to work, it was just too boring. Terry used his connections and helped me land a job as a roofer. It was hard work, but much better than working at the feed lot. I worked as a roofer for two summers.

Prior to the start of fall football practice, my friend Mike Crawford and I would work out hard to get in football shape. We had an organized routine that helped us get in the best possible shape. It proved to be very hard for me. After roofing all day, it was very difficult to lift weights, train, and run two miles, but I did the best I could.

Right before fall practice, I met with my counselor. We put together my short- and long-term education objectives and then I registered for classes. My major in college was physical education. I declared speech as my minor. My uncle Marvin was a teacher and a coach, and I thought I'd follow that career path.

When the football season began, wearing number 77, I started at defensive tackle on the freshman football team. We played a full six-game schedule and we went 5–1. When the freshman season ended, the entire team continued to practice with the varsity squad to get experience and help them prepare for their games.

In high school, I was the best football player on the team. I excelled on the field. But in college, every player on the team was equally talented or better. It didn't take me long to figure out that I might not be able to play professional football. It wasn't that I didn't have the desire or toughness. It was my lack of speed. I had to work out harder over the next year to get faster.

After football season, I focused on my studies and getting into better football shape. I went to all my classes and did pretty well. Every Thursday night, even during the football season, I went to the wrestling matches in Amarillo. I would drive the eleven miles from campus to the arena. I never had to pay and was always welcomed into the venue by the boys. I would then watch the Funks, Dick Murdoch, Ricky Romero, Cyclone Negro, and Jack Brisco. Though I was smart to the business, I still got excited watching their matches.

During my freshman year, I pledged with a fraternity—Alpha Tau Omega, which was founded by Otis Allan Glazebrook. The ATOs on campus were like the characters in the movie *Animal House*. We were the party guys. There was never a shortage of beer. Jeff Lloyd was a fellow brother and we became good friends. We were the biggest guys on the freshman football team. During initiation, the brothers tried to haze us, but they couldn't because we were so big and tough. They wouldn't dare do anything weird. Once Jeff and I became members, however, we did some hazing of our own. I remember us tying some nerd pledge to a pole in the middle of the night. It was all in fun.

Shortly after the conclusion of the football season, I ran into an old friend, Ricky Romero's son, Ricky Jr. He worked at a clothing store in the Amarillo Mall. One day, Ricky said, "Ted, there is a girl working at the store that says she knows you. Do you know a Jaynet Foreman?"

"Yeah, I remember her. I've known Jaynet since the sixth grade."

A few days later, I went to see Jaynet at the clothing store just to say hello. We ended up going to lunch and relived some old times. I eventually asked her out. We started dating just before Christmas.

When classes resumed in January, I focused on three things: school, working out, and Jaynet. I really enjoyed being with her, but I could still hear my dad's voice: "Remember, Teddy, you can't stay focused with a girlfriend." I knew he was right, but I was determined to make it work.

In the spring of my freshman year, I made another friend: Tully Blanchard. He transferred from Southern Methodist University. In order to play quarterback, Tully came to West Texas State. Tully and I immediately befriended each other. We had a lot in common. Like me, he was the son of a former professional wrestler; his father was Joe Blanchard.

TULLY BLANCHARD:

I arrived at West Texas State in the fall of 1974. Earlier that summer, Teddy got injured during two-a-days and missed the season. When my dad wrestled for Kansas State, he wrestled Teddy's dad, who was a star athlete at the University of Nebraska. They became friends and both went on to become professional wrestlers. Because of these ties, Teddy and I quickly became friends and remain friends today.

Though he was a good football player, his injuries affected his performance. Unfortunately, good football players get hurt. Since he was going to miss another year of football, Teddy decided to start wrestling. You couldn't blame him, and it was a good decision. I had actually started training to wrestle in the off-season and had refereed for three years prior to attending West Texas State. Teddy and I even had a few workouts together at the Amarillo Sports Arena.

Ted was a great professional wrestler, in the top 10 percent of all time. He had great success and drew a lot of money every place he went. There were very few people that were equal to him in ability.

When spring football practice came around, I had a decent session. Jerry Barons was the defensive line coach and I was determined to impress him. Though I was tough enough, my lack of speed was still hurting me. I did all the drills the coaches required and squatted a lot to build up my legs. I had to get faster. One time while running wind sprints during practice, one of the coaches jokingly said, "DiBiase, we are going to have to get a sundial to start timing you."

It was at that time that my interest in professional wrestling peaked. I made up my mind that I wasn't going to stress about not being able to make it in professional football. If I made it, fine. If not, I was going to become a professional wrestler.

Back in the day, there were no wrestling schools. The only way you got into professional wrestling was growing up in it; either that or somebody brought you in. Since both those scenarios applied in my case, Dory Funk Sr. had no problem with me working out in the ring. I did this in between roofing and spending time with Jaynet.

The ring was permanently set up in Amarillo at the sports arena. Any spare moment I had, I would go and take bumps and learn the fundamentals. I worked out in the ring with Steve Romero, Ricky's son. Steve would later go on to wrestle as the legendary Jay Youngblood.

That summer, I also met Tomomi Tsuruta. "Tommy" was an amateur Olympic wrestler from Japan who'd signed on with Giant Baba's All-Japan company. Baba had sent him to the Amarillo territory to be trained by the Funks, and Steve and I would work out with him. Since the Funks were his teachers, Steve and I would participate in the workouts. I was taught how to bump and lock up, as well as headlocks, armbars, and other basic moves. Tommy would later wrestle and star in All-Japan under the name of Jumbo Tsuruta. He is often recognized as one of the strongest and toughest wrestlers in the history of All-Japan.

We were picked to win the Missouri Valley Conference my sophomore year. I was six-four and weighed in at 250 pounds. I wasn't good enough to start, but I got a lot of playing time. We had a horrible year going in, 3–7. A lot of people attributed the losing season to Coach Mayfield. Even though he knew how to coach and created a powerhouse at Permian High School, he was treating college players like high school players.

When football season ended, I unequivocally knew that I was still lacking speed. I spoke to Coach Barons about the reality. He said, "Ted, you are as aggressive as anybody on the team. But what you are lacking is speed." So I committed myself to working out harder than ever before to overcome my deficiency.

At the time, my relationship with Jaynet was escalating. Every spare minute I had was with Jaynet. We were in love. A few weeks after the end of football season, on December 21, 1973, Jaynet and I married. It was a small wedding at a Roman Catholic church in Canyon. A lot of my fraternity brothers and friends, Terry and Vicki Funk, and a few other wrestlers attended, as well as all of Jaynet's immediate family. After the reception, we went to Willcox, where my family met my new bride.

When we returned to Canyon, Jaynet and I moved into a small off-campus apartment. Jaynet was working and going to school. During the afternoons, I did my off-season training with the team. I would come home to visit with Jaynet and get something to eat. I would then head back to the gym and work out some more. I got in really good shape.

Prior to the start of spring football practice, Coach Barons called me into his office. Sitting with him was the offensive line coach. "Ted, here is what we are going to do this spring. Because of your lack of speed, we are going to make you an offensive tackle. How do you feel about it?" Though deep down I preferred playing defense, I said, "If it is going to help me start, then great."

I had a fantastic spring practice, and it showed on the field. I picked up the assignments rather quickly and was blowing people off the line right and left. I did so well on the field that I was scheduled to start at right tackle when the season started in the fall.

TITO SANTANA:

Ted and I played football together at West Texas State. He was a year behind me, we belonged to different fraternities, and I didn't really get to know him too well until we both worked together in the Amarillo territory, and I got to know him much better in World Wrestling Federation.

I wasn't a wrestling fan growing up. It used to come on TV real late in South Texas, so I didn't know anything about the business. I only knew of Terry and Dory Funk because they used to come out and watch us practice. At West Texas State, Teddy would show everyone how tough he was by cracking beer cans on his forehead. I thought he was nuts for doing it in the first place, and sometimes his forehead would bleed. After a while, I realized his main goal was to become a professional wrestler.

The following Thursday night, Jaynet and I went to the wrestling matches. The night was special because the NWA World Heavyweight Champion, Jack Brisco, was in town. Jack was a babyface in Florida, but when he came to Texas he wrestled as the heel. That night he was going to defend his title against former world champion Dory Funk Jr. Some of the best wrestling matches I ever witnessed were between Dory Funk Jr. and Jack Brisco.

After the show, Jaynet and I met Terry and Vickie at some honky-tonk bar on Amarillo Boulevard. Dory Jr. was also with us. Back then, we had to kayfabe—protect the business. So Terry and Dory stayed in character when Jack Brisco came into the same bar. He sat with some other heels on the other side. Though he couldn't sit with us, out of courtesy Terry and Dory sent him complimentary beers.

As the evening wound down, some drunk cowboy asked Jaynet to dance. I stepped in and said, "Sorry, fella. She isn't going to dance with you. She is my wife."

The drunk didn't care much for my intervention and said, "I'm not talking to you. I am talking to her."

I was pissed. "Well, I'm talking to you. I just told you to take a hike, pal. She is not going to dance with you, she is my wife!"

The liquored-up cowboy reached over and grabbed a chair. As he swung it at me, I blocked it and decked him right between the eyes. The punch sent him across the room. He fell on his back right between Jack Brisco's legs. To make sure he didn't get up, I jumped on top of the guy and started pounding his face in. In between punches, I said to Jack, "Hello, Mr. Brisco. I am Ted DiBiase. It is a pleasure to meet you."

9

REFEREEING AND WRESTLING

A few weeks after spring football practice ended, I started working as a lifeguard at the city pool. I quit my job roofing because I needed both the energy and the time to work out. I also had to make some more money. Now that I was married, it was important that I help Jaynet with the bills. That year, the NCAA changed one of their rules, which now allowed me to earn some extra cash.

The NCAA had a policy that restricted college athletes from participating in professional sports. If you violated the rule, the NCAA would strip you of your scholarship. Fortunately for me, the NCAA adjusted their policy so that someone could now work in a sport other than the one for which they were on scholarship. The ruling allowed me to take another job: as a professional wrestling referee.

One day I was at home studying when the phone rang. It was Terry Funk. He said, "Hey, Teddy. What are you doing?"

"Nothing much, just hanging out and studying."

"We need a referee in Lubbock tonight. Bring a pair of white pants. I'll have a referee shirt for you. I'll pick you up in fifteen minutes."

To say I was nervous would be an understatement. I knew how to bump and the basics, but I had never refereed before or even been in front of a live crowd. On the way to the fairgrounds in Lubbock, I had a thousand questions for Terry. Dick Murdoch was also in the vehicle.

I was asking Terry and Dick question after question. And they weren't answering. I was getting frustrated, but back then that was the way you learned the business. They simply threw you out there. Finally, Terry said, "Teddy, you know the rules, don't you?"

I said, "Yeah."

"Ten-count on the floor, ten-count on the apron, five-count to break on the ropes, et cetera. Just go out there and do it."

TERRY FUNK:

I was Teddy's mentor. When he got into the business, we would put him in the backseat and ride with the front seat pushed all the way back. Before he was accepted in the business, he had to pay a price. I always got on him regarding what to do and what not to do. He always listened and respected what I and others said. Teddy had a respect and understanding of the business.

I was still nervous when we got to the arena. I was told that the first match I would referee was the opening match between Mike Paducis and one of Ricky Romero's sons, who was under a mask. As I walked to the ring and climbed through the ropes, it dawned on me: this was where my dad died. His last match was in this building, in this ring. For that entire day, up until I climbed into that ring, I didn't think anything about my father's death. But when I stepped into the ring, it was like Dad had passed me the torch.

When the matches concluded, everyone in the back told me I had done a good job. I loved it and had a great time. Terry paid me fifty dollars, which was a whole lot more than the $2.30 an hour I was making as a lifeguard. Terry dropped me off home later that night.

Let me tell you about Dick Murdoch. In the late 1960s, Dick had formed a tag team with Dusty Rhodes called the Texas Outlaws. They had a very successful run, but Dick was now making a name for himself in the Amarillo territory. Dick went on to wrestle around the world for some thirty years. In 1996, he died of a heart attack at forty-nine.

I had gotten to know Dick from hanging out with the guys after the matches on Thursday nights. I was in college and didn't have lots of spending money, so Dick would always take me out and buy me a beer. He would say, "Don't worry, kid, I got you covered." He treated me like a younger brother. Over time, I developed an admiration for Dick Murdoch, and he served as one of my mentors in the business.

One night in January of my sophomore year, Jaynet and I were sound asleep. About two-thirty, we heard banging on the front door. I got up to see who it was, and it was none other than Dick Murdoch. "It's me, kid, open the door." As I opened the door, I noticed Dick had his pickup truck backed up to the front door. "I got you a wedding present, kid." He and his buddy unloaded a thirty-inch color television.

I was at a loss for words. Back then, a television set that size must have cost five hundred dollars. I thanked Dick. As he headed out the front door he said, "Kid, I wouldn't be showing that TV off to too many people. It's a little warm."

"You didn't steal it, did you?"

He coyly replied, "I didn't. But the guy I bought it from did. I got it for fifty dollars."

As my sophomore academic year came to a close, I learned a little more each night about the wrestling business. I refereed more and more. Refereeing

Dick Murdoch.

became my second summer job, after lifeguarding. I was learning so much from being in the ring. I learned a lot about the psychology of wrestling before I ever actually wrestled a match. I appreciated the opportunity to be the only other person in the ring as two wrestlers went at it. Not only was I learning, I had the best seat in the house.

Although I was doing a good job refereeing, I was still very green. One Saturday morning in Amarillo, Andre the Giant was scheduled to wrestle on television against the top heel in the territory, Cyclone Negro. I was the special referee for the match. Prior to the match, I was confused about the ending. They kept changing the finish and I was still unclear about the outcome. Before I knew it, the match was under way.

Near the end of the match, Andre did something and covered Cyclone Negro. His shoulders were down and I counted one-two-three. On live television, Andre had just pinned the top heel in the territory. I had just screwed up the angle they were shooting. To cover my error, Terry Funk ran into the ring and immediately attacked Cyclone Negro. They then started fighting outside the ring. To get Cyclone's heat back, Terry was slammed through a table. Terry saved the top heel in the territory. When I got to the back, they lit into me pretty good. I tried to explain and in the end we all had a good laugh about it—thanks to Terry Funk.

In June of 1974, I was refereeing a match that featured Jim (J.J.) Dillon. Dillon was one of the most hated heels in the territory. When he lost the match, he felt that it was my fault. Out of the blue, he punched me and knocked me out. This set up my first ever wrestling match. In a six-man tag match, Terry Funk, Dick Murdoch, and I beat J.J. and the Patriots (Robert Griffin & Bobby Hart). J.J. and I later met in a few singles matches.

Though most people remember J.J. for being the manager of the legendary Four Horsemen, he was a very good professional wrestler. Like me, he started in the business as a referee. He was also a heck of a nice guy and I learned a lot from being in the ring with him. I enjoyed watching the many classic battles in the territory between him and Dick Murdoch. When I worked in World Wrestling Federation, I ran into J.J. He worked in the front office and was part of the creative team. J.J. is now retired from professional wrestling. In 2007, I had the honor of being inducted by J.J. into the Professional Wrestling Hall of Fame in Amsterdam, New York.

J.J. DILLON:

I first met Teddy when I was wrestling in the Amarillo territory. Since he was the son of the legendary "Iron" Mike DiBiase, I immediately respected him. But Teddy wasn't a full-fledged wrestler at that time. He was still a junior at West Texas State University on a football scholarship. But he was very interested in the business, so Terry Funk got him started as a referee.

After a while, Teddy decided to start wrestling. As one of the top heels in the territory, I helped launch Teddy's wrestling career. After I lost a match that Teddy was refereeing, I beat him up. Terry Funk came down to his rescue. This led to Teddy's first match, which was actually a tag match between me and someone, against Teddy and Terry. After that tag match, I wrestled against Teddy in his second-ever match.

Even at that point, he was a natural. He was a great athlete and, because of his father, had a tremendous amount of respect for the business.

Later that summer, Terry told me that they needed someone to fill in for one of the wrestlers. He had got hurt and they needed a quick replacement. I rode with Terry to El Paso. I didn't wrestle that night as Ted DiBiase. They put me under a mask and I went against Japanese wrestler Akio Sato. He led me through it. During the course of the match, Sato went to do a specific move. Well, he went the right way and I went the wrong way. In the end, I separated my shoulder.

I don't know what hurt more, my shoulder or the fact that I was looking at two-a-day football practices that were about to begin in two weeks. When Terry found out about my injury, he was beside himself. "Teddy, do not tell your coaches you were wrestling. They will be mad at you, and even madder at me!" I told the coaches I had fallen off a trampoline while working out.

TERRY FUNK:

When Teddy first started in the business, he didn't do it for the money. He loved it and it was in his blood. He learned from his mother and father. When he first got in the business, the Million Dollar Man could have been bought very cheap: he worked for five dollars a night. In fact, he would have even paid to be in the wrestling profession.

I quit refereeing and wrestling. I focused all of my energy on rehabilitating my shoulder. When football season started, I pulled a hamstring. I was trying so hard to practice at a high level with the shoulder injury. At the same time, I started having pain in the big toe of my right foot, and I didn't know what was causing it. My buddies on the team started busting my chops because of all the tape I required before leaving the locker room. Between my shoulder, hamstring, and toe, they started calling me the mummy.

The pain in my big toe wasn't going away, and the team doctors were stumped as to why the toe was not healing. I was sent to a specialist. After numerous tests, it was revealed that I had gout. Gout is when there is an excess of a particular acid in the body that settles into the joints. The foot is a common resting place, which explained why my toe was always hurting.

BILL WATTS:

I met Teddy when he was playing football at West Texas State. It was the last year that the University of Tampa had a football team. He didn't play in that game because he had gout. I remember teasing him about how in the world could a twenty-year-old already have gout!

Due to my injuries, I played on and off throughout the season. I played the entire season hurt. I was very disappointed: I had been all excited about being the starting tackle, but it didn't happen.

The season ended and I put even greater pressure on myself to get ready for spring football practice. I knew that I had to have a great spring practice to attain a starting position for my senior year. I worked out hard and overcame all my injuries.

Unfortunately, right at the start, I suffered another injury. As I planted my feet to block a defender, the offensive guard to my left was blocked into me in such a way that he fell onto me. As we both fell to the ground, I could feel his weight come down on my left knee. A sharp pain ran through my left ankle and knee. The doctors said that I had stretched the ligaments in the knee and severely sprained my ankle. It was unstable and loose, and I had to go to rehab to make sure my bones stayed in alignment and regained their normal range of motion. I started rehabilitation but never finished spring football practice.

One night after the matches, I had a conversation with Dick Murdoch. "Teddy, I have a great idea. Instead of you staying here refereeing, how about you find out if you really want to be in the professional wrestling business? Come to Louisiana this summer and wrestle." I liked the idea, and because of the new NCAA rule, I was eligible to do it.

Dick was leaving the Amarillo territory and was headed to Bill Watts's Mid-South promotion. "Teddy, I'll talk to Bill Watts and get you in there. Wrestle this summer and see how it goes. You will make better money than anything else you can do." I had met Bill Watts and was impressed, so I accepted Dick's offer. The plan was to wrestle all summer in the Mid-South territory and return to West Texas State to finish my senior year.

The next day, Dick Murdoch picked me up and took me to meet Bill Watts. On a handshake, I was working for Bill. Wanting to be like my dad, I wrestled as a heel that summer. I was the opening match every night.

My first match in the Mid-South was a televised match against Danny Hodge. I don't remember much, only that I was scared to death. Danny sensed it and said, "Just listen to me, kid, and you will do fine."

Danny was one of the greatest amateur wrestlers our country has ever known. While at the University of Oklahoma, he won the NCAA title three times and went undefeated. He had a 46–0 record, with 36 pins.

At the end of the summer, I called Coach Mayfield and told him I wasn't coming back. I quit the football team.

When I returned to Amarillo, many of my friends urged me to return to school for my senior year. Even Terry and Dory Funk Jr. told me to stay in school. But I had a good feeling about being in the wrestling business. I felt very comfortable in the ring and I was making a decent living. I had no interest in going back for my senior year and riding the bench the entire football season. Jaynet supported my decision. In September of 1975, we headed to Baton Rouge.

In hindsight, dropping out of college was one of the worst decisions I ever made. I regret it. Don't get me wrong, I love the wrestling business. But college was something that I started, and never finished. I failed to follow through on my goal.

TERRY FUNK:

I was against Teddy going into the business at that time. He had a full scholarship and I wanted him to finish his education. I saw the advantages of getting a degree. Teddy could have something to fall back on.

I always felt that Teddy leaving early had a lot to do with Dick Murdoch. Dick didn't see why it was necessary to have an education. He came out of the school of hard knocks and only wanted to be a professional wrestler. Dick was a great guy, teacher, and wrestler, yet he couldn't see anything beyond wrestling. Even though Teddy wanted to wrestle full-time, I suggested that he go back to West Texas for his final year.

Bill Watts was a very big and burly man and I was initially intimidated by him. He was very savvy and in full control of the task at hand. Bill reminded me of great football coaches—like Vince Lombardi and Bill Parcells—he would yell and scream, wanting the task to be done right. But he never challenged you out of hate or spite. He had high expectations and wanted everyone to improve and learn.

BILL WATTS:

I knew Teddy's father very well. Mike was incredibly classy and I had the utmost respect for him. Because of our relationship, I already had a soft place in my heart for Teddy. Since Teddy came from a wrestling family, I gave him the benefit of the doubt that he respected the business. And he did. He was a credit to the business.

The Mid-South wrestling territory was owned by Bill Watts and Leroy McGuirk. It encompassed the states of Mississippi, Louisiana, and Oklahoma. The major cities included Shreveport, Jackson, New Orleans, Tulsa, and Oklahoma City. Some of the smaller cities were Lafayette, Greenville, Fort Smith, Monroe, and Alexandria.

Bill was the promoter and booker. He had one of the greatest minds and understood the psychology of the business. Leroy was a former wrestler, but Bill pretty much ran the company. Mid-South had some of the biggest and toughest wrestlers in the business: Bill, Dick Murdoch, the Masked Assassin, the Spoiler, Stan Hansen, and Bob Sweetan. Eventually, Bill bought out Leroy.

In 1975, I was grossing roughly $350 week. It was just enough to pay my bills. There was no insurance, retirement, or health benefits. I was even responsible for all my expenses, including transportation, gas, and lodging. I easily put sixty thousand miles on my car that year. Some guys put on a whole lot more than that.

I was also responsible for my own meals. Back then, healthy eating was not a major concern. There was no emphasis on having a great body in professional wrestling. If you had a chiseled body, fine. You were a wrestler. You were supposed to be athletic and look the part. Everybody was different and it was important that you looked like your character. You were supposed to mirror society, so the fans could relate to you.

It was all about bulk eating and eating cheap. Chicken breast and a baked potato was not part of my diet. There was no time for fine dining. The boys and I would look for the cheapest and best buffets, as well as the local supermarkets to load up on bread and lunch meats. I remember many a night eating bologna sandwiches (bologna blowouts).

The Mid-South territory had a demanding schedule. I worked seven days a week. My weekly schedule started in Shreveport, Louisiana, on Saturday morning for TV tapings. I would then hop in the car and drive three hundred miles to Greenville, Mississippi, for an evening match. To save money and wear-and-tear on vehicles, most guys carpooled. I would then spend the night with the boys in the cheapest hotel we could find. Sometimes we would sneak three or four guys into one hotel room. It was called "heeling." We would "heel" the room. Two guys would sleep on the mattress and two guys on the box spring.

I would then get up early the next morning and drive another three hundred miles to Houma, Louisiana. I'd have to be there at least an hour before the show, so I'd grab some food and get a workout. After my match, I would drive another three hundred and fifty miles to Shreveport and spend the night. Then I would get up early in the morning and drive another three hundred and fifty miles to Tulsa, Oklahoma, and wrestle that night. The next morning, I would drive back to Shreveport. That routine would continue for months and seemed endless.

Every Saturday, Bill would give me my bookings. At the time, I was a curtain-jerker and would wrestle the first or second match every night. I was as green as the grass, so there was no need for me to be at the TV studio for Wednesday interviews. I still went to the studios in Shreveport as much as possible to watch. I watched and learned from "Killer" Karl Kox and Dick Murdoch. I wanted to gain as much knowledge as I could. The business was a brotherhood and I savored the camaraderie.

Since Dick Murdoch brought me into the company, I traveled and spent most of my time with him. My daily routine with Dick consisted of beer and more beer. After each show, we would stop and get a case. If there were four of us in the car, we would have two cases. It's amazing that no one got into any major accidents or received any DUIs.

Of all the towns we wrestled in the Mid-South territory, my favorite was New Orleans. I loved the shops, restaurants, people, and the bars. Murdoch asked me, "Have you ever been to New Orleans?"

"No."

"Are you telling me you have never been to Bourbon Street? Oh, I have to take you to Bourbon Street."

One night in New Orleans before the matches, Dick walked up to Grizzly Smith and pointed my way. "Griz, the kid has never been to Bourbon

Street. Do you mind if I borrow your car tonight to show the kid a good time? You can catch a ride back to Baton Rouge with one of the boys and we will meet up in the morning." Without hesitation, Grizzly said, "Sure."

Grizzly was Bill Watts's right-hand man. He was the company's match-maker and road agent. He was Bill's eyes and ears and was responsible for what happened at the event.

Grizzly is a great guy and a former wrestler. He was part of a successful tag team with Luke Brown known as the Kentuckians. He is also the father of professional wrestlers Jake "The Snake" Roberts, Sam Houston, and Rockin' Robin.

After the matches, we headed out to New Orleans in Grizzly Smith's 1974 yellow four-door LTD. Before we even got onto I-10, Dick pulled into a 7-Eleven and got a six-pack of beer. The first place Dick took me was the world-famous Felix's Restaurant and Oyster Bar. The restaurant was located in the heart of the French Quarter. It was a very crowded and noisy place. It was also where I was introduced to raw oysters.

Dick ordered a few dozen oysters and lots of beer. The oysters re-minded me of snot and I wasn't too interested in eating them. But Dick edu-cated me on how to do it properly: scoop it out of its shell, place it on a cracker, top it with horseradish and cocktail sauce, eat it, then wash it down with a cold beer. The cracker gave the oyster some texture, which made it eas-ier to eat. I must have downed about a dozen.

After about an hour, Dick and I took a walk down Bourbon Street. We grabbed a few more beers and took in the sights. I was twenty-one years old, and I was overwhelmed by the town and excited by its energy.

Dick then took me to Pat O'Brien's on St. Peter Street. We walked through an old carriageway entrance and into one of the most magnificent restaurant bars I had ever seen. It was huge, with beautiful architecture, a piano bar, restaurant, and other amenities. Dick took me directly to the bar and ordered me their world-famous drink, the Hurricane. It's a sweet drink with a little fruit syrup and lots of rum. Dick and I must have drunk three or four before heading back to Bourbon Street. Before we left, I went to use the restroom.

I was standing at the urinal and that was when I started to feel green about the gills. I was drunk. I staggered out of the restroom and walked up to Dick. "Dick, unless you want to carry me back to the car, I suggest we leave now."

Laughing, Dick said, "Okay, kid, let's go home." I later found out that Dick had known the bartender at Pat O'Brien's. After my first Hurricane, he had the bartender kick up the alcohol content on the next three.

As we headed back to the car, Dick and I saw all the hot dog carts along Bourbon Street. There must have been one on every corner, and Dick insisted that we stop at every one. We would stop at one and buy one with just mustard. We would then walk another block and get another with chili. A few more blocks and we would get one with cheese and onions, along with a cold beer to wash it down. Talk about gluttony.

We finally made it back to the car and headed to Baton Rouge. Dick was driving and country music was blaring on the stereo. I was trying to sleep but Dick kept waking me up. "Kid, don't let me fall asleep." I kept dozing off, and Dick kept slapping me to keep me awake.

As you can imagine, summertime in New Orleans is very humid. That particular morning was no exception. The car didn't have an air conditioner, so we were sweating buckets when Dick asked me to "put on the 490 system."

"Where and what is that?"

"Roll all four windows down and I'll do ninety!"

We had an eighty-five-mile drive in front of us. Dick was doing ninety miles an hour on the interstate. It was about two-thirty in the morning. As we crossed the expansion bridge over Lake Pontchartrain, we got a flat tire. We pulled off to the side of the road. Both of us got out and opened the trunk to get the jack and spare tire. We took the jack out and attempted to hook it to the bumper. It was dark and we didn't have a flashlight, so we couldn't see where to hook the jack to the slit in the bumper. We did our best. Somehow we managed to get the car elevated, and though it was wobbly, I took the hubcap off and started loosening the lug nuts. Dick yelled, "Get away from the car, it's about to fall." I jumped back as the car fell off the jack, and as I did so, I hit the hubcap and all the lug nuts went flying onto the interstate.

There I was on my hands and knees crawling on I-10 looking for those lug nuts. Dick kept yelling at me to get out of the road, and I'd holler back, "If we don't find the lug nuts, we're going to be here all night."

"Get up and get over here! Somebody is coming." I paid no attention because I was determined.

As I was crawling around, my eyes met two black shiny boots. I looked straight up and saw a badge. It was a Louisiana State Highway Patrolman. As he stood there with his arms crossed over his chest, he looked down at me and said, "What the fuck are you doing!?"

In all sincerity I looked up and said, "Well, sir, I am looking for my nuts!"

He cracked a smile and said, "Get your ass out of the road before you get killed."

The officer's presence was a blessing, because the lights from his car allowed us to find the lug nuts and to see what was wrong with the jack. After Murdoch explained the situation, the officer shined his flashlight at the bumper. Lo and behold, Dick and I obviously had no idea how to work the jack. We thought a piece of the jack was missing, but we had failed to place the jack in the hole of the bumper. The officer properly affixed the jack and I changed the flat. The officer then told Murdoch to drive slowly and to be very careful. Fortunately, the highway patrolman let us go without issuing us a ticket.

As we headed back down the interstate, my heart was still racing. I was nervous because of what had just happened and I was hoping that we didn't have any more car trouble. My hands were filthy and it was hot as blazes. Dick was now driving about a hundred miles per hour and my head was pounding. All of a sudden, my stomach started hurting. I could feel the beers, liquor, oysters, and hot dogs churning. I begged Dick to pull over. I told him I was sick and not feeling well. "Oh, kid. You aren't sick. It's mind over matter. If you don't mind, it doesn't matter. I am not stopping. If you are that sick, just stick your head out the window." So I stuck my head out and heaved for what seemed like an eternity.

It was roughly four o'clock in the morning when we arrived at the hotel in Baton Rouge. We got out of the car. We could see that from the door to the back fender, the car was covered in my vomit. I was worried. Dick said,

"Don't worry about it. Get some sleep and in the morning we will clean it up before Griz comes and picks it up." The next morning, I had a heck of a hangover, so I took a few aspirin. I looked outside and saw that Griz's car was spotless. The mess on the car had been washed away by a hard rain that hit the area while we were asleep. I told Dick and we were both ecstatic.

BILL WATTS:

Because we made long road trips, drinking was a way of life in our business. My territory was so brutal to travel, and drinking was one way to pass the time. It was a way to stay awake and give one something to do. Teddy also came into the business with Dick Murdoch. Dick was a huge beer drinker. Since Teddy was traveling with Dick, I am sure he was drinking a lot of beer. I mean a lot of beer.

After showering and getting dressed, we looked the car over to make sure everything was in proper condition. While inspecting the vehicle, Dick and I noticed that the back bumper had a huge gash in it. Our poor jacking job earlier that morning had created a huge ten-inch gash. Dick and I vowed to tell Grizzly the truth and to pay for the damages.

Grizzly showed up and Dick and I apologized. Dick was truthful and told him the entire story from our time on Bourbon Street, to the police officer yelling at me to get out of the road, to me heaving out the window along I-10. Surprisingly, Grizzly started laughing his butt off. As Grizzly was getting ready to leave, we reaffirmed that we would pay whatever it cost to get the bumper fixed. Grizzly looked at both of us and said, "Nope, I'm not fixing it. I am going to leave it just the way it is." Puzzled, Dick and I looked at each other and then simultaneously asked Grizzly, "Why?"

"Because every time somebody asks me how it happened, I am going to tell them the story!" And he left it at that.

Another time in Baton Rouge, I was so exhausted that I checked into this run-down hotel slightly off the interstate. I went into the room and hit the sack. A few minutes later, I went to the bathroom. To my chagrin, there was no toilet! I called the hotel office to ask for another room. The attendant said, "Well, sir, the only room I have available is one with a toilet but no television." I replied, "Man, it is four a.m.; I don't need a television but I need a toilet!"

Because of my demanding schedule, I barely saw Jaynet. The business was starting to put a strain on our marriage. I had no business being married at the time. Often, I conducted myself like I didn't even have a wife. We were both immature and I was married to the business. I was wrestling every night of the week and poor Jaynet would just stay at home doing nothing. She was bored out of her mind.

About two months after arriving in Shreveport, we moved into another apartment. We had hoped that would afford us an opportunity to see more of each other. It didn't. A month or so later, we decided to separate, and she relocated back to Amarillo. There, at least, Jaynet would be close to her family and friends.

From the late fall of 1975 to the summer of 1976, I worked and traveled throughout the Mid-South territory. Whenever I got two days off, I would drive back to Amarillo to be with Jaynet. The travel was wearing me out. Something had to give.

My first year as a full-time professional wrestler was a learning experience. Bill Watts, Dick Murdoch, Grizzly Smith, and others taught me a lot. I learned about respect for the business, the psychology of the sport, organization and punctuality, self-discipline, and sacrifice. Their guidance made me yearn to learn even more, and to strive to get better.

In professional wrestling, there is a certain protocol. You respect the veterans of the business and yield to their expertise. At times, I would sit in the dressing room and not say a word. I would speak only when asked. I understood my role and knew that it was those senior wrestlers who paved the way and gave me the opportunity to be part of the greatest sport in the world. It was their business and I would pay my dues to earn their respect.

My first angle was with "Killer" Karl Kox. He was the biggest heel in the Mid-South promotion, and in my opinion, he was one of the greatest heels ever. Karl had mastered the psychological part of professional wrestling. Mur-

"Killer" Karl Kox.

doch had been in an angle where Kox "blinded" Murdoch, which sidelined him indefinitely. Since I was a protégé of Murdoch—who was the biggest face in the business—Bill Watts decided to parlay Murdoch's injury into my first angle in the territory.

In a manner that only Bill Watts could stir up, I went out to the ring to help an injured Danny Hodge, who had been pummeled by Kox prior to the start of their match. On the way back to the locker room, with Danny over my shoulder, Kox kicked me. Mad, I offered to take Danny's place in the match. The fans thought I was crazy, because a young babyface like me stood no chance against the brutish and volatile "Killer" Karl Kox. Eager to destroy me or anyone, Kox laughed and accepted the match.

It was a ten-minute match, and Kox destroyed me for the entire match. But, because he was overconfident, I was able to sidestep him and hook him for a quick pin. Kox couldn't believe it. A rookie just pinned the top heel in the territory. He was furious!

The following week, Kox told a television audience that he had underestimated me. He demanded a rematch, but there was a special caveat: he would give me ten thousand dollars if I could last ten minutes in the ring with him. The fans begged me not to accept the match. But I was determined. Once the match started, the people couldn't believe that I was wrestling smart and simply trying to avoid a furious Kox. He chased me around the ring as I stalled for time. The object of the match was not to beat Kox, but to last ten minutes. In the end, I was beaten and exhausted, but ten thousand dollars richer.

It seemed as if the fans knew that there was no way I could beat Kox. They were even more surprised that I had lasted the entire time. The angle was popular and the television ratings went up. Because of the angle's success, the bookers decided to prolong it, but added a new twist.

The next time, Kox raised the ante to fifteen thousand if I could last twenty minutes. I once again stalled and tried to outsmart him. It worked for about ten minutes. Then, Kox completely annihilated me for the remaining ten minutes. With about one minute remaining, the fans gasped as Kox placed me in his patented finishing hold, the Brain Buster. I landed on my head. The crowd was dead silent. Nobody had ever kicked out of his finisher. Kox arrogantly covered me, but I unexpectedly kicked out on the two-count and rolled out of the ring. Kox couldn't believe it. As he complained and griped to the crowd and referee, the bell rang. Time expired. Though I was on my knees outside the ring, I was fifteen thousand dollars richer.

Kox and I continued the angle one more week until Murdoch returned. It was during my final battle with Kox that I juiced, or cut myself, for the first time. Since I had never juiced before, I was going to let Kox do it for me.

However, during the course of the match, I overzealously rammed my head into the ring post. Blood was everywhere. The following week, lo and behold, I once again hit my head on the outside ring post's metal turnbuckle. That gash required stitches.

BILL WATTS:

I can never forget the first time Teddy was going to juice. He was so nervous that it was hilarious. During the course of the match, he somehow split his head open when he rammed it into the ring post while almost knocking himself out. I teased him that he wasn't getting paid double for that juice. The next week, with stitches in his head, Ted had to juice again. Sure enough, the same exact thing happened.

Throughout my career, nobody juiced me. I did it myself. Prior to a match, I would drink some bourbon and take a few aspirin. This would help increase the blood flow. I would take a disposable razor and slice off maybe a one-inch piece of it. To conceal the blade, I wrapped it in a piece of athletic tape. Most guys kept the razor blade either in their trunks or under the athletic tape on their wrists or fingers. I simply kept it in my mouth. I placed it at the bottom of my lip like a dip of snuff. I never had a problem.

One summer night after wrestling in Lafayette, Louisiana, I was scheduled to do a run-in. I waited at the door of the dressing room for my cue. I was only wearing my corduroy jeans and cowboy boots, and I had a towel around my neck. At the time, I used to go commando—no underwear. As I ran to the ring to do my spot, I went to leap up on the ring. However, because of the humidity, I slipped on the way and ended up doing a split on the floor, sliding completely under the ring; so much for my rescue. I was embarrassed but I quickly got up and ran back into the ring to save the day. Everyone was laughing. I also noticed that it was quite breezy. When I fell down, I apparently split my pants. Everything was exposed for the crowd to see. Thank goodness I had my towel to cover up.

In mid-1976, I left the Mid-South promotion. I had been away from Jaynet for a while and though I was still married, I was engaging in many youthful indiscretions. I knew what I was doing was wrong. So I called Jaynet and I told her everything. The next morning, Jaynet was at my front door. She had driven all night. We spent all morning and afternoon crying, trying to understand. In short, we decided to patch it up. So to save my marriage, I decided to go back to wrestling in the Amarillo territory.

10

GAINING EXPERIENCE IN THE BUSINESS

In the early summer of 1976, I returned to the Amarillo area to repair my marriage. Prior to my return, I called Terry and told him I was coming back. My good friend and mentor was now the NWA World Champion. He was wrestling all over the country and the world. The NWA acknowledged one true world champion, and that person was recognized throughout all the various territories and the world. It was an honor to know that my mentor was indeed the champion of all champions.

Wrestling for All-Japan Pro Wrestling.

TERRY FUNK:

Teddy is a great kid. Though he isn't a kid anymore, I will always call him kid. He has a wonderful heart. In the ring, he always got his share, and always gave his share to his opponent. He always wanted to do what was best for the promotion, not himself. His heart was always in the right place. His father had a lot to do with his upbringing. Ted's father was my mentor and I was Teddy's. I consider it an honor to be called Teddy's mentor.

As the champion, Terry wrestled in every territory—Florida, Kansas City, Amarillo. The champion wrestled as a heel wherever he went, except in his home territory, so Terry was a babyface when he came home to Amarillo. The champion would usually wrestle the top babyface in every territory. He might wrestle an hour every night.

Terry told me that things had changed since my last stint in Amarillo. Dory Funk Sr. was no longer the promoter. He died when I was in college. Dory Jr. and Terry were wrestling outside the territory, so the promotional duties were left to their uncle, Herman Gust. He was a great guy, but didn't have the knowledge to properly run a wrestling promotion.

I noticed a major difference between the Amarillo territory and the Mid-South promotion. It wasn't run or organized well. Things were much smoother in the Mid-South. Business was also not as good in Amarillo. I believe it had a lot to do with Terry and Dory Jr. not being there to handle the promotions.

A few weeks after I settled in with a now pregnant Jaynet, Terry came home for a few days. We chatted and he asked me if I was interested in wrestling overseas. I jumped at the opportunity. In August of 1976, I went on a five-week tour with Giant Baba's All-Japan Pro Wrestling promotion. I was there with some other American wrestlers, including the legendary Bobo Brazil. He was the senior American on the tour. Other workers on the trip were Big Red, Tank Patten, and the "Wolfman" Willie Farkus.

I was guaranteed a thousand dollars a week. They paid for my airfare, hotel room, and transportation. The only thing I had to pay for was food. Upon arrival, they gave me a two-hundred-dollar advance. The dollar was strong: three hundred yen to the dollar—sixty thousand yen was equivalent to two hundred dollars.

Wrestling in Japan was very different from wrestling in the States. Whereas in the States I had to drive everywhere, with All-Japan the only thing I had to do was hop on the bus. All-Japan had two nice Greyhound-type buses—one for the foreigners and one for the Japanese guys. The buses took us everywhere. I also traveled by ferry and bullet train—a train that goes two hundred miles per hour.

My first trip to Japan was unbelievable. I was amazed by how clean the cities were. Tokyo, the most populated city in the world, sparkles. Unlike our major cities, there isn't any graffiti on the walls or trash littering the streets. The people take pride in their communities and treat them with the utmost care and respect. They also have a lot of respect for older people and people with authority.

It was the first time in my life traveling outside the United States. Besides my admiration for the Japanese people, I took a liking to their food and spirits. I wasn't a sushi lover at first, but now I really enjoy it. Some of my other favorites were beef and chicken curry rice, Korean barbecue, and spaghetti with meat sauce. It wasn't like Grandma's, but it was okay.

Here I am with some of my youngest fans.

I loved the beer that was easily available from vending machines. I also liked sake.

One day riding on the bullet train, out of boredom, Bobo Brazil taught me how to play spades. As we were playing, Bobo broke out this giant bottle of sake. Bobo asked, "Hey, kid, you want some sake?"

"Sure."

For the remainder of the trip, Bobo and I were sipping sake. I didn't think anything of it, and then all of a sudden the wine just started to sneak up on me. By the time we arrived at our destination, I was drunk.

For most of my young wrestling career, I was a babyface. In Japan, every worker who isn't Japanese is called *gaijin* and works as a heel. The first night in Japan was reserved for television tapings. I was scheduled to wrestle in a tag-team match with my partner, Bobo Brazil. As a kid, I watched Bobo Brazil wrestle. He stood at about six-four and weighed about 280 pounds. He was a great man and was very popular with the fans in the States.

As we waited in the dressing room, I asked Bobo, "Since I have never been over here before, is there anything I need to know or do?" In wrestling, it seems like everything is a trial by fire. Nobody tells you anything. You just have to go out there and experience it for yourself. Bobo said, "Kid, just do what I do. Follow my lead."

About ten minutes before our match, someone brought Bobo a bucket of water. He stuck his head in it, then dumped the water all over his body. Bobo's hair was all messed up and he was soaking wet.

As we made our way to the ring, Bobo turned into this madman. He started pounding his chest and making loud and scary sounds. The fans scattered. Although Bobo wanted me to follow his lead, I didn't feel I could, so I just walked behind him.

It was customary for the flower girls to give each wrestler a big bouquet of flowers and then bow to them as they got into the ring. We both accepted our bouquet. But all of a sudden, Bobo started eating his flowers and spitting them out. Though Bobo had told me to "follow his lead," there was no way I was going to eat the flowers. Out of the corner of my eye I saw some of the Americans standing out in front of the dressing room. They were all standing out there laughing their butts off. The rib was on me. It was my first match in Japan and Bobo had set me up real good.

Another thing about Japan that I noticed was how different it was. There was no cursing or screaming. The Japanese fans just sit there and watch the match very quietly. You would get light applause only after a high spot or special move.

The wrestling style in Japan is very different from the United States. It is more of a rugged style and the workers are very stiff. The matches were half-shoots and no one gave any wrestler anything. You had to earn the respect of the wrestlers and the fans.

On the tour, I wrestled my old friend from my college days in the Amarillo territory, Jumbo Tsuruta. We had a great match in front of a packed crowd. It was very technical. We had a great story, battled back and forth, and had a great contest. That match helped me earn respect among the Japanese wrestlers.

After five weeks in Japan and another five thousand dollars, I was ready to come home to see Jaynet.

When I got back to the States, I wrestled a couple of months in the Amarillo territory. Because of my friendship with Harley, I got connected with Bob Geigel and Pat O'Connor in the Kansas City territory. They offered me an opportunity to wrestle, and I took them up on it.

I wrestled in Kansas City, also known as the Central States territory, from the winter of 1976 to August of 1977. Harley Race was one of the owners of the Central States promotion, along with Bob Geigel and Pat O'Connor, both of whom I befriended. My father had been very good friends with all three.

I bunked with the boys, including "Bulldog" Bob Brown. Bob was originally from Canada and spent ten years wrestling in the Central States territory. He was a heck of a nice guy and we had lots of good times together. I also bunked a few times with Pat O'Connor and Harley Race. Three things about Harley will always stand out: he was a great wrestler, an awesome friend and person, and someone who could drink lots of beer.

HARLEY RACE:

One night after a show in San Angelo, I got Teddy a "little under the weather." The next morning we had to fly out of Amarillo to Kansas City for television. When we arrived at the hotel early that morning in Amarillo, I called Bob Geigel and told him that Teddy might not be there for television and it was my fault. Little did I know, Teddy somehow managed that morning to catch a flight to Kansas City and made the television tapings.

Kansas City was a great learning experience for me. My first angle was with Bruiser Bob Sweetan. Bob was a very good wrestler. He was a major heel, and his style reminded me a lot of my dad's. We had many good matches together. I also managed to capture the Central States heavyweight title from Sgt. Slaughter.

BOB GEIGEL:

Teddy was a very good-looking kid and enjoyed life. He was full of energy and enthusiasm. When he was with Murdoch, the two of them tore up the town. They were a wild twosome. But he was a great wrestler. I wanted Teddy in Kansas City for many reasons, but three stand out: (1) he had lots of TV exposure; (2) he was a good-looking young guy with lots of ring savvy; and (3) he just had a lot of natural ability. He learned fast and never had any bad matches. When Teddy was in the ring, he was always exciting. He was a benefit to the territory.

Since Jaynet was three months pregnant, I was very concerned about her living in Amarillo and convinced her to move to Kansas City. In March of 1977, we moved into a nice two-bedroom apartment. But she was unhappy. Since she was pregnant and we were still trying to work on our marriage, I decided to move back to Amarillo with her in August of 1977. Once again, I went to work with the Amarillo territory.

On September 10, 1977, my son was born. We named him Michael Wills, Michael after my father and Wills after my biological father. At twenty-three years old, I was a proud father. I was at Jaynet's side throughout the delivery. To see the birth of my own flesh and blood was truly a blessing. With both of our families in attendance, we later baptized Michael in the Catholic Church, with Terry and Vicki Funk as his godparents.

Harley Race was now the new NWA World Heavyweight Champion. Harley was making his rounds in the Amarillo territory. I was being pushed as the top babyface in the territory, and as such, I was granted a title shot. To build up my match, I went to a live TV interview with Michael in my arms. The announcer asked me, "Ted, why do you want to be the Heavyweight Champion?"

Looking down at Michael I replied, "There are lots of reasons why I want to be the Heavyweight Champion, but I am holding the most important—"

"And who is that you're holding?"

"This is my son, Michael. He is my father's namesake. I want to be the father to him that 'Iron' Mike was to me!" It was straight from my heart. It also struck a chord with the crowd—the event sold out.

Harley and I wrestled to a one-hour time-limit draw. We put on one great match. It was tit for tat and we kept the fans on the edge of their seats for the entire hour. I went on to wrestle him at every major town in the territory. It was a great learning experience for me. I was thankful that Harley was such a great person who did whatever he could to make me look good in the ring.

Wrestling in the Amarillo territory gave me an opportunity to be closer to Jaynet and Michael. I was happy to be home and grateful to get the chance to be back with some of the boys—Ricky Romero, Ervin Smith, Johnny Weaver, Rip Hawk, Merced Solis, and Swede Hanson. Terry and Dory Funk Jr. were also back and Art Neilson became the booker. Art had great ring psychology and knew how to book, so the promotion started to improve.

But the territory was every bit as demanding as the Mid-South region.

People need to understand that although we were celebrities, and were seen on TV, the life was extremely difficult. Here is a typical week: Saturday morning was reserved for local television taping in Amarillo; immediately after TV, I would drive 350 miles to either Pueblo or Colorado Springs to wrestle Saturday night; after the match, I would drive 350 miles to Albuquerque; I would wrestle in Albuquerque and drive back to Amarillo Sunday evening—900 miles in two days; Monday morning I would drive 260 miles to Abilene for an evening match; that evening I would drive 100 miles to Odessa; after wrestling that night in Odessa, I would drive another 100 miles to San Angelo; after that Wednesday evening match, I'd drive 300 miles back to Amarillo; Thursday night was reserved for wrestling locally in Amarillo; and on Friday, I would drive 100 miles to Lubbock for a Friday evening match. When it was over, I would drive back to Amarillo, catch a few hours of sleep, and then begin the whole routine all over again with Saturday morning television tapings.

Merced Solis was my former teammate at West Texas State University. He was a tight end and had been drafted by the Kansas City Chiefs. He was cut in training camp but later played in the Canadian Football League. He didn't like it there, so he decided to try professional wrestling. Merced and I would eventually become Western States Tag Team Champions. When he went to World Wrestling Federation, he became known as Tito Santana.

I also teamed with Ervin Smith. He was a great athlete and amateur wrestler, and he even played football at the University of Tampa. When Ervin first broke into the business, he worked in Florida. He made decent money and the trips were short. He was home every night. They had spoiled him. When he came to Amarillo, Ervin was overwhelmed by the long trips. The three-hundred-plus-mile trips were too much for him. When he left the Amarillo territory, he quit wrestling.

Ervin was a great guy but he had a temper. One night in San Angelo, we were in a tag match against Brute Bernard and the "Angel" Frank Morrell. Those two guys were some of the most repulsive heels around—they were the two ugliest heels in the territory. During the course of the match, the four of us were fighting outside of the ring. Back then, the only thing separating the fans from the wrestlers was a thin piece of rope. The rope was attached to a pole with a steel base.

All of a sudden, Brute picked up a pole and went to hit Ervin in the stomach. As Brute came down with the pole, one of the fans interfered and disrupted Brute's motion. The fan was actually trying to help Ervin, but instead the tugging on the rope caused the base to swing upright. The steel base went right across Ervin's eyelid, slicing it wide open.

Ervin's quick temper was now in full bloom. Sensing it, I dove down on Ervin and shoved him under the ring. I lay on top of him and tried to calm him down. As I was keeping him down with my body, I had to keep my hands on my head, because he was pounding me as he tried to get up. Ervin was screaming, "Let me go. I am going to kill that son of a bitch." He finally calmed down and we finished the match. We ended up laughing about it over a case of beer that night as we drove back to Amarillo.

We had television interviews the next day. Ervin was a good wrestler but he got very uptight when being interviewed. During the interview, he pointed to his stitched eye and said, "You see this, this just . . ." He stumbled with what to say. Finally he said, "This just fuckin' pisses me off!" He walked off the set, slamming the door on the way out. Everybody busted out laughing.

Ervin had a very nice Grand Prix. For us wrestlers, a good radio and sound system was very important. So he got a special sound system installed. They didn't install it properly, so he took the car back in. After he bickered with the manager, they finally fixed the problem. That night, I rode with Ervin to Lubbock. My younger brother, John, had come to visit, so he came along for the ride.

After our match at the Coliseum in Lubbock, we stopped at a nearby convenience store and loaded up the cooler with a case of beer. John was sitting in the backseat next to the cooler, so he was designated as the bartender. As soon as we left the parking lot, Ervin turned on the radio. It was dead. He tried adjusting the controls and lightly tapped the dash, but nothing. Out of the blue, Ervin yelled out in frustration and punched his windshield with his right hand. The windshield shattered. You should have seen the look on my brother's face.

Not a word was spoken for what seemed like an eternity as we headed down the road. I could barely see out of the windshield, so I asked Ervin, "Can you see okay?" He finally cracked a smile and said, "Give me a beer."

JOHN DIBIASE:

When Teddy got in the wrestling business, I would travel as much as I could with him. I always looked up to him. He was a great athlete and I wanted to emulate him on the football field. He was also an excellent wrestler. I respected him and he was a role model for me.

I was hired to make an appearance in the movie *Paradise Alley*. The star was Sylvester Stallone. The plot involved three Italian brothers living in Hell's Kitchen, New York, during the 1940s. Each brother used his personality to help the others in their wrestling careers.

Terry Funk was also featured in the movie as the maniacal Frankie the Thumper. Besides myself, there were over a dozen guys there, including Dick Murdoch, Bob Roop, Gene Kiniski, Ray Stevens, Dory Funk Jr., and Al Perez, to name a few. I had a part in only one scene in the entire movie, the montage. If you blinked, you would miss me. Stallone was a nice guy and treated me very well. Sly said, "I believe that these professional wrestlers are the best improvisational actors in the business."

To be in the movie, I had to get a Screen Actors Guild card and was paid five hundred dollars a day, plus room and board. It was the easiest fifteen hundred dollars I ever made. I also received royalties from the movie. For fifteen years or so, I received a nominal check in my mailbox. I would spend the fifteen or twenty dollars on toys for my kids.

Mike London was the promoter in Albuquerque. He was a tough guy with his trademark eyebrows, goatee, and mustache. He simply looked like the devil. He was also an alcoholic. One night, I was in the main event wrestling Harley Race for the NWA world heavyweight title. Mike stood in the center of the ring and called for the microphone so he could introduce the contestants. He introduced me to a sold-out crowd. Then it was time for Mike to introduce Harley. "His opponent, weighing in at two hundred and fifty pounds from Kansas City, ladies and gentlemen, your NWA World Heavyweight Champion . . ." He had forgotten Harley's name. Mike put his hand over the microphone, looked over at Harley, and said, "What's your name?"

Embarrassed, Harley cocked his head and mumbled, "Harley Race." And that concluded the introduction.

As Mike was leaving the ring, some guy at ringside caught the error and proceeded to say something smart. Mike looked at the fan and, with an open microphone so the entire building could hear, said, "This is my goddamn town and I can do any fuckin' thing I want!" I'm sure the people never forgot that incident.

Shortly thereafter, the Funks sold their promotion to Dick Murdoch and Blackjack Mulligan. Terry and Dory Jr. didn't want to be tied down and were clearly making more money traveling to other places. Although Dick was my friend and unequivocally a great wrestler, he wasn't a good promoter. The same can be said for Mulligan. Business was down and the territory wasn't doing as well as in the past.

To make money, I continued going to Kansas City. Bob Geigel and Harley Race liked my work and they continued to book me. My angle with Bob Sweetan was over and I was making decent money. I was making a name for myself and picked up lots of exposure. St. Louis was a wrestling hotbed, with some of the best talent in the business.

In early 1978, all my hard work finally paid off. Sam Muchnick, the promoter in St. Louis, gave me an opportunity to work in his territory. St. Louis was like a one-city territory. It was its own entity. The talent that came into St. Louis was from all over the country.

The paydays in the St. Louis territory were much better than most places. I was making about four to five hundred dollars a week wrestling in Amarillo. When I went to St. Louis, I would average that much a night. If I was fortunate enough to be in the main event, which I was a few times, I would get paid close to six thousand a night.

BOB GEIGEL:

The St. Louis territory was effectively promoted by Sam Muchnick. Sam was president of the National Wrestling Alliance for many years. I also served as president for about four years. Verne Gagne, Pat

O'Connor, Harley Race, and I eventually bought the territory from Sam. We wanted Teddy in the territory because of his great work ethic and in-ring psychology. He was never selfish in the ring and an absolute class person in the dressing room.

Soon thereafter, Sam came up with an idea that would give me more exposure than I'd ever had before in my wrestling career. Sam knew that Harley and the DiBiase family had a great history and that he could build up the match. He said, "What if you were to wrestle Harley Race for the NWA Championship?"

I ecstatically replied, "That would be fantastic!"

In March of 1978, at the famous Kiel Auditorium in St. Louis, Harley and I wrestled in the main event to a one-hour time-limit draw. I didn't win, but the match gave me the exposure I desperately needed to move to the next level. I knew that if I performed well in St. Louis, then I would have many opportunities to wrestle in the larger markets such as New York City. Sure enough, in April of 1979, Vince McMahon Sr. inquired about my availability.

HARLEY RACE:

At one point in Teddy's career, he was in line to become the NWA Heavyweight Champion. We had many good matches together in St. Louis. He had all the skills to become a heavyweight champion. He was very athletic and extremely smooth in the ring. Despite losing his father at an early age, Ted achieved success in the same profession that took his father's life, and that speaks volumes about his character. He was a man's man.

I was very fortunate to be part of World Wide Wrestling Federation. At the time, they were known as the "big body" territory. Some of the guys that worked there were Bruno Sammartino, Pedro Morales, Ivan Putski, Andre the Giant, and Superstar Billy Graham. Their champion was Bob Backlund. I was young and had four years of wrestling experience, but I knew I was a solid enough wrestler to make it in the territory. I was in great condition, but I didn't have a very muscular physique. I was always told to work out and look athletic, but to not overdo it by looking like a muscle head.

Vince liked my work and brought me in as both a babyface and the North American Heavyweight Champion. Jaynet, Michael, and I moved into a two-bedroom apartment in Parsippany, New Jersey. It was a forty-five-minute drive to New York City.

It was the first time there had ever been a champion in WWWF besides the heavyweight and tag-team champions. I didn't actually beat anybody. It was part of the angle to introduce me to the territory. There was no explanation where the title came from or how I had won it. Vince's agents treated me very well and I learned a lot from Angelo Savoldi, Arnold Skaaland, and Gorilla Monsoon. It was also the first time I'd met Vince McMahon Jr.

At the time, Vince's son worked exclusively as an announcer. The only time I saw Vince was when I'd wrestle at Madison Square Garden and at the television interviews and tapings in Allentown and Reading, Pennsylva-

At Madison Square Garden, wrestling Pat Patterson.

nia. We always got along and he conducted himself in a very professional manner.

In the Mid-South territory, the main champion held the North American Heavyweight Championship. When I got to New York, I told Vince that there was a problem with the angle. Being the class act that he was, and not wanting to step on Bill Watts's toes, a few weeks later he had me dropping the title at a TV taping to Pat Patterson. To change the name of the title, the company made up a story about Pat Patterson going off to some international tournament. Pat put up the North American heavyweight title to enter the tournament in Rio de Janeiro, Brazil. He won it all, unifying the North American Championship with the South American Championship to create the Intercontinental Championship. Pat was then crowned the first ever Intercontinental Champion.

PAT PATTERSON:

I had just come to New York as a heel and Teddy was this good-looking babyface. The first time we wrestled was at a TV taping in Allentown. The fans were really into him. I beat Teddy using a pair of brass knuckles and it almost caused a riot. Teddy and I put on such an excellent and fast-paced match, which was in direct contrast to the slow-moving matches the fans were used to at that time.

But the one match I will never forget was at Madison Square Garden in 1979. It started my career in World Wrestling Federation and I still think about it quite frequently. We wrestled in the main event on the card. We had a great match and wrestled up until the Madison Square Garden's curfew—which was eleven. We did everything right going in and out of the ring, near fall after near fall, and you could feel the ring shaking from the crowd stomping their feet. The crowd went absolutely insane. I beat Teddy right before the bell went off to retain the new North American Heavyweight Champion title.

I always liked Teddy. He was a fun guy to be around and was always happy. He was also good for the business. Win, lose, or draw, he could have a great match anywhere. He was entertaining the people and doing everything right.

The move to World Wide Wrestling Federation offered me a tremendous opportunity to both get more exposure and wrestle in front of packed houses in some of the grandest venues in the country: Philadelphia, D.C., Boston, and New York. I will never forget the first night I wrestled at Madison Square Garden—then and now the ultimate wrestling venue in the world. At twenty-five years old, I attained more notoriety and made more money than ever before.

Wrestling in WWWF was different than the Amarillo and Mid-South territories. First, the wrestling wasn't as stiff. Moves, punches, and spots weren't as snug. Also, the drives weren't bad. Most cities were within 150 to 200 miles. I still worked every day, but I was home almost every night.

I had come to the territory with Tito Santana. A great friend, Tito lived in a nearby apartment complex, and he later met his future wife in the same town.

TITO SANTANA:

When Ted and I first arrived in New York in 1979, we traveled everywhere together. We also got lost a lot. One of our first shows together was in Long Island. We couldn't find the Van Wyck Expressway or Southern Parkway. When we stopped and asked for directions, nobody knew anything or wanted to help. Ted and I were two Texas boys and people were a lot friendlier back home. It didn't take us long to figure out that nobody trusted anyone and people just didn't want to talk to us.

During my run, I had singles matches against Pat Patterson and the Iron Sheik, and tagged with Tito Santana, Ivan Putski, and Andre the Giant. I enjoyed working with Pat Patterson because he was so knowledgeable. I learned a lot of ring psychology from him and did everything he told me.

The Iron Sheik and I had a few good matches. It was about the same time as the U.S. hostage crisis in Iran. At a match in Pittsburgh, the Iron Sheik was getting booed. He was beating the tar out of me. But the tough, blue-collar crowd was so loud that the "USA, USA" chants were deafening. As the fans kicked up the noise and got behind me, the Sheik looked at me as if he was getting scared of the crowd. He said to me in his Farsi accent, "I don't think I beat you tonight, brother!" I put him at ease the best I could and the match continued. He ended up pinning me as planned.

The Iron Sheik and I used the crowd's energy to fuel our matches.

Andre and I had been friends since we met while I was in college. He always called me "boss" and we had a lot of great times together. Andre was one of those guys that either liked you or didn't. Fortunately, he took a liking to me. But Ivan Putski wasn't as lucky. Andre didn't like him.

One night in Providence, Rhode Island, Andre, Ivan Putski, and I were scheduled to be in a six-man tag against the three Valiant Brothers—Jimmy, Johnny, and Jerry. Before the match, Andre came up to me in the locker room. "Hey, boss. Tonight, you tag me. You tag nobody else!"

I said, "Okay." Throughout the entire match, Andre made sure that I never tagged Putski. I'm sure Putski figured it out, but what could he do to the seven-four, four-hundred-and-fifty-pound giant?

After a match at the Boston Garden, Andre, Tito Santana, Arnold Skaaland, and I headed to the hotel bar after checking in. All four of us were sitting at the bar drinking. Andre decided to challenge me to a drinking game. "I tell you what, boss. You get five shot glasses and you can put whatever you want in them: beer, whiskey, water, milk, whatever. I will get five large glasses filled with beer. We'll line them up, five shots for you and five beers for me. I'll bet you I can drink all five of my beers before you can drink five shots. If I win, you buy everybody a round. If you win, I'll buy everybody a round."

I looked at Arnold and Tito. I knew full well that I couldn't outdrink Andre. But I only had five small shot glasses to his five twenty-ounce beer glasses. I could certainly drink those faster than he could. "Okay, Andre, that's a bet."

"Now, don't mess around. The only rule is that you don't touch my beer glasses and I don't touch your shot glasses."

"Okay, that's fair. Let's do it."

The bartender poured whiskey in my five shot glasses and Andre got his five beers. Arnold was the referee. As soon as he said go, Andre had inhaled one beer as I had finished my fourth shot. After he finished his first beer, he turned his glass upside down and placed it over my fifth shot glass! Since the rules stated we couldn't touch each other's glasses, there was no way I was going to get my fifth shot. I shook my head in disbelief and Andre casually finished his four beers. Then with a smirk he said, "Kid, buy a round for everyone."

Another night after wrestling in Portland, Maine, Andre, Tito, and I went back to the hotel. We had a few drinks in the bar to wind down. We then headed up to Andre's room to drink some more and play his favorite card game, cribbage. Andre was good and he never lost. After a few hours of playing, we decided to head down to the nearby Denny's to get something to eat. I basically had to carry Tito, because by then he was three sheets to the wind.

We each ordered breakfast, and before our meals arrived, Tito just dozed off right there in the booth. The waitress finally brought the food and set our plates down. Andre and I finished, but Tito was still out and hadn't touched his plate. With a smirk on his face, Andre reached over and took Tito's plate. He put half of the food on his plate and the other on mine. Andre quickly put the plate back in front of Tito and we ate his food. Andre inserted a knife in one of Tito's hands and a fork in the other. Then he pushed Tito. "Wake up, it's time to go." Half asleep, Tito looked down at his plate and hands. He then looked up at us and asked, "Was it good?"

I love New York City. When I first flew into New York from Amarillo, I was overwhelmed by the size of it all. To me, after having lived in Willcox, Omaha, Baton Rouge, Kansas City, and Amarillo, New York was a concrete jungle. But I loved the attractions, food, people, and entertainment. My only regret was that I never went to the top of the World Trade Center.

At a television taping in Pennsylvania, I was there when Terry Bollea (aka Hulk Hogan) showed up for the first time. Hogan was bigger than life and was unbelievably ripped. It was the first time that Vince Sr. had laid eyes on him. Terry wasn't there to wrestle, but to meet and greet Vince Sr. The kid from Tampa had long blond hair, a deep tan, and an incredible body. You could see the dollar signs in Vince's eyes. Hogan came into the territory as a heel and he was assigned a manager, Freddie Blassie.

In December of 1979, I left. I only spent eight months in WWWF, but time had passed. They had given me the opportunity and let me have a run of it, and now it was time for me to go. I wasn't the physical specimen they wanted. In spite of my work, I didn't stand out. I didn't have a gimmick. Chief Jay Strongbow was a great guy and had a big influence in my life. He told me, "Kid, you have to have a gimmick." I never had one. I was just Ted DiBiase.

I was scheduled to wrestle my last match in Madison Square Garden against Hulk Hogan. At that point, Hogan wasn't a big star. It was actually his first WWWF match and his first at the Garden. I knew Vince Sr. wanted to make a star out of him. Before the match, I went up to Vince. "I know you really want to get Terry over. What would you like for me to do?"

Vince's response made me feel really good. "Teddy, you do it any way you want to, because I know you will do it right." Vince's confidence in me assured me that he believed in me and knew I was up to the challenge.

Terry was a heel back then. Hogan and I had one heck of a match, and he earned his first victory at the Garden. After the match, he thanked me. A few years later when Terry came through the Mid-South promotion to wrestle a few shots for Bill Watts, we saw each other in the locker room. He walked up to me and we shook hands. Winking, Hogan said, "Brother, I owe you one." He still remembered the night that we had the match at the Garden and what I had done to help him get over.

The next day, the family and I headed back to Amarillo for the Christmas season.

11

TAKING THREE STEPS

I contacted Bill Watts and returned to the Mid-South in January of 1980. I rented an apartment in Baton Rouge and once again began the grueling Mid-South road schedule. In late February, I defeated Mike George in Shreveport to capture the North American title. Mike was a mainstay with the NWA and worked in various territories. We had a great match that night. I would work on and off for Bill Watts over the next seven years.

With all the moving around, not to mention our immaturity,

That's me with Michael Hayes.

my marriage to Jaynet had deteriorated. We decided to get a divorce; it was amicable. Even though Michael lived full-time with her, I could see him any time I wanted. In February of 1980, I drove Jaynet and Michael to the airport, where they flew to Amarillo to stay with her parents. Saying good-bye to Michael was the hardest thing I had ever done. It about killed me.

For the next six months, I stayed in Mid-South wrestling and tried to get my personal life back in order. Terry Funk, Bob Geigel, and Harley Race all advised me that I should leave the Mid-South and go to the Atlanta territory. Atlanta was the home of Georgia Championship Wrestling as well as the Superstation, TBS. I could get national television exposure. TBS was the only cable network that carried wrestling throughout the whole country. I was told that they were pushing for me to become the next NWA World Heavyweight Champion. I was overwhelmed by having such an honor bestowed upon me. It made me work even harder.

TERRY TAYLOR:

I first met Teddy while working the Georgia territory. I had only been in the business six months and was extremely green. Teddy was just so nice to let me ride with him and tried to help me with my work.

When we were together in the Mid-South territory, I remember Teddy was supposed to get a shot at Ric Flair for the NWA heavyweight title. But he was heading off to Japan, so an angle was crafted to open the door for me to wrestle Flair. During a match, Dick Murdoch attacked Teddy beforehand. Dick gave him a Brain Buster on the concrete floor. Teddy proceeded to bleed over everything. It was the bloodiest thing I had ever seen.

Before I left Mid-South, they told me not to say anything about being pushed to become the NWA Heavyweight Champion. The other territorial promoters were pushing for two other guys, Dusty Rhodes and Ric Flair. The decision to crown the next NWA champion was a political decision. Bob told me that he would talk to Sam Muchnick and the others. I was advised to just work hard in the ring and to keep everything on the down low. While in Atlanta, I was to simply get over with the fans and get as much television exposure as possible.

It was in October that I relocated to Atlanta. Jim Barnett was the promoter. He was openly homosexual and rumor had it he was one of Rock Hudson's lovers. Ole Anderson was the booker. Ole was real stubborn but I got along with him. Other talents that came in and out of the territory were Jake

Roberts, Jim Duggan, Terry Taylor, Dusty Rhodes, Tommy Rich, Tony Atlas, Ronnie Garvin, Steve Keirn, Terry Gordy, Michael Hayes, and Bob Roop.

JIM DUGGAN:

Right after playing football for the Atlanta Falcons, I had my first ever meeting with Teddy in a tag match. As soon as I locked up with Teddy, he let out a curse word and immediately tagged in his partner, Tommy Rich. I was extremely green and very stiff. Sensing that I was out of control, Teddy wanted nothing to do with me in the ring.

I really enjoyed wrestling and hanging out with Michael Hayes. I have known Michael some twenty-plus years. I worked with him in the Mid-South, UWF, and Georgia territories. He was the vocal leader of the Freebirds' faction and was unquestionably a great ring psychologist. Because of his understanding of the business, he is currently one of the major creative producers and writers in WWE.

But that doesn't mean Michael was a great in-ring wrestler. He was quite stiff and he frequently potatoed me. We must have wrestled a hundred matches, but our Strap match in Fort Worth stands out. We had a very stiff match. It was nothing personal. It was just Michael being Michael in the ring. And this time he had a strap in his hand; he about beat me to death.

MICHAEL HAYES:

Teddy was born to wrestle. He was a consummate professional in the ring. Teddy had great appeal with the fans and he was someone they could put their arms around. When he turned heel, he had the fans' attention. Before he was the Million Dollar Man, he was a star in his own right in the Mid-South, Georgia, and UWF.

The wrestling industry as a whole is a lot better off for having Teddy DiBiase in it. His passion for the business is one of his most redeeming qualities. I know my life is better because of Ted DiBiase.

The Georgia territory did really well the year before I got there, but I was coming in on the tail end of the success. I was earning decent money, but nothing great. I continued my St. Louis and Kansas City trips to supplement my income and to increase my exposure.

Since business was down in Georgia, Ole got disgruntled and eventually quit. Robert Fuller was brought in to take his place. Robert was a decent guy, but I had already been exposed to one of the best bookers in the country, Bill Watts. Robert was no Bill Watts.

The first day I walked into the Atlanta studios, Austin Idol came up to me and said, "Hey, Ted, nice to see you. When are you getting the title?"

"What are you talking about?"

"You know, the world heavyweight title. That's why you're here, right?"

"I don't know what you're talking about." Idol just smiled and walked away. I don't know who, but somebody had let the cat out of the bag. In wrestling, nobody can keep a secret. The big joke in the business is that there are three forms of communication: telegraph, telephone, and tell-a-wrestler.

TERRY FUNK:

Teddy was a major performer and was seriously being considered for the NWA heavyweight title. However, Dusty Rhodes and Ric Flair had bigger organizations and more power behind them. In the end, Teddy lost out.

BOBBY "THE BRAIN" HEENAN:

I first met Ted working the St. Louis territory. He was a big guy with a great voice and was a good wrestling talent. He was very nice and personable. The buzz was that he was going to be the next NWA Heavyweight Champion. I thought he would make a great champion.

Because of the talk of me getting the title I got on Jim Barnett's bad side. He thought I was running my mouth, but I wasn't. There was no way I was about to blow the opportunity to capture the title. But one night in Kansas City, somebody asked me how things were going in Atlanta. I honestly replied, "It's terrible. The booking is horrible!" Word eventually got back to Jim, and he wasn't too happy.

In retrospect, I should have kept quiet about the booking. But I turned out to be right. Jim told Robert that I was in line for the title and to book the matches so that I could get over with the crowd. However, Robert was more concerned about getting himself over with the fans. He started booking matches with me and him working as a tag team. We started running an angle against Plowboy Frazier and someone else. Plowboy—later known as Uncle Elmer—was an atrocious wrestler. He would whine and cry, and did very little in the ring because he was worried about getting hurt.

Fuller was eventually replaced by Buck Robley. I knew Buck when he worked for Bill in the Mid-South, and he could book and tell a story. He knew I could work and he liked me a lot. I had some programs with Ronnie Garvin and Buzz Sawyer. Buck wanted to help me. He told me that I had heat with Jim, and he wanted me to do what I could to get Jim's boy, Tommy Rich, over with the crowd. Buck teamed me with Tommy in a program against the Freebirds. The angle was designed to get the fans to dislike them while getting us over. It was one of Buck's better angles.

During a live television match, Terry Gordy of the Freebirds threw me out of the ring. He proceeded to give me three piledrivers on the concrete floor. I started shaking and was bleeding from my mouth. An ambulance was called and I was strapped to a gurney and rushed to the hospital. The cameras never stopped running and the show ended with the legendary announcer Gordon Solie telling the national viewing audience, "Ted DiBiase has been taken to Piedmont Hospital here in Atlanta."

Late that afternoon, the switchboard at the hospital was about to crash.

People from all over the country were calling to check up on me. It was so overwhelming that the staff even asked me for a list of people who I wanted to speak to. I accidentally left Jim Barnett's name off the list. When Tommy Rich came to visit he told me Jim wasn't too happy and to put him on the list. The rift between me and Jim widened.

I spent a week at the hospital and never said a word about the injury being a work. The company paid for everything, including my salary. There wasn't a single thing wrong with me, but I still received numerous gifts, flowers, and letters.

The doctors and nurses checked on me every day. I went through therapy, received massages, and had numerous X-rays and tests. After seven days, the doctors told me they couldn't find anything wrong, but were stumped because of the bleeding. I was released and told to come back if any more bleeding occurred. I never said a word and protected the business.

What happened was that in the locker room before the match, I had drawn some blood and placed it in a balloon. I kept the balloon in my mouth until I was piledriven outside the ring. I then punctured the balloon with my teeth and spit out the plastic for the referee to retrieve.

After spending the week in the hospital, I spent another three weeks working, but not inside the ring. They started doing interviews to build up my comeback: in the hospital, in therapy, at my apartment, in the gym getting in shape. On April 26, 1981, I finally made my return to the ring in a match with Tommy and me against the Freebirds at the Atlanta Omni.

All the towns I wrestled in were within driving distance of Atlanta. Since the trips weren't long, I would go home every night. Every Saturday morning we did TV tapings and interviews in Atlanta. Other towns we wrestled in included Columbus, Carrollton, Marietta, Griffin, Augusta, and Macon.

STEVE KEIRN:

When Teddy came to the Georgia territory we quickly became friends. He was a great guy and had a lot of respect for the business. We rode together throughout the territory and got to know each other real well. What I also liked about Teddy was that he was a fast driver. It was very important that we got to each town early and on time. To leave as late as we could was the objective of the day. Teddy had a lead foot. He could easily make the one-hundred-or-so-mile trip from Macon to our residences in about an hour.

I rode everywhere with Steve Keirn. He and I got along real well. He had a beautiful Weimaraner dog named Elton. He was married to a wonderful woman and owned a house in the Stone Mountain area. After renting an apartment in the metro Atlanta area for three months, I eventually moved to his side of town.

STEVE KEIRN:

There is no doubt that Teddy was a tremendous worker. But he was quite naive at times, which made it pretty easy to rib him. I never pulled any serious ribs on Teddy. One of my goals back then was to be one of the best ribbers ever. Ted always used to tell the boys, "Don't rib Keirn, because when he ribs you back you are going to hate it worse than anything."

One time, I had an opportunity to call some spots to Teddy when we were working against each other. I called a long, high spot to Teddy. He was trying so hard to get it that he kept repeating it back and forth to me. It started off with a one-tackle drop-flat, then a hip toss, a couple of armdrags, a slide out on the floor, then chase me around the ring and back in. To hear Teddy trying to repeat it back to me was amusing. Well, the spot never got past the drop-flat. Once I hit Teddy with the tackle and he dropped flat, I dropped on Teddy's back right in the middle of the ring. Now Teddy, who was concentrating on the high spot I had just called, was caught off guard. It took him a second or so to realize that I had just pulled one on him. All of a sudden he started to laugh, which caused me to chuckle in front of the audience, and the entire time I was still lying on his back. He never took any of the ribs seriously and laughed just as hard at himself as anybody else would at him.

I was single and partying like there was no tomorrow. My one-bedroom apartment was the ultimate bachelor pad. Since I was home almost every night, I frequented all the bars and dated lots of different women. I also got to know my downstairs neighbor, Tony, really well. He and I became friends. Unfortunately, Tony introduced me to cocaine. I never abused it, but if it was available, I did it. It was very expensive and there was no way I was going to waste my own money buying it. I'm embarrassed by it today, but the truth is that I did use. It was one of the dumbest things I had ever done.

On April 26, 1981, the same day as my return to the Omni after my one-month rehab from my so-called neck injury, I met Melanie.

I was at the apartment pool working on my tan with my friend Scott and his girlfriend, LuAnn. It was roughly noon, so I had about six hours to kill before the show. While putting on tanning oil, out of the corner of my eye I saw the most beautiful girl I had ever seen. It felt like a lightning bolt had hit me. LuAnn even had to push me out of my stare. I watched Melanie all afternoon without saying a word. I wanted to meet her, but she was obviously with a date. Eventually, I psyched myself up to go back down and chat with her.

I went back to the pool and chatted with some friends while keeping my eye on the prize. Before I could say anything, her date introduced himself to me. He pointed at the bombshell who was now staring at me and said, "Ted, there's a young lady over there who would really love to have your autograph." I was nervous, but I calmly called to her, saying, "Well, come on over here. I'd be glad to give you an autograph."

After an introduction and some small talk, Melanie and I proceeded to the manager's office for a pen and paper. On the way, she said, "So what's it like to be an Atlanta Falcon?" A lot of football players lived in the complex and surrounding community. I was surprised, but judging by the look on her face, she was dead serious. I explained to her that I wasn't a football player but rather a professional wrestler. "You're a *wrestler?*" We laughed. On a piece of paper I wrote, "To Mel, the best-looking girl at the pool, for sure."

"This is going to cost you."

"What do you mean?" In the end, I managed to get her phone number and we said our good-byes. I then went back to the apartment to change for my return match that evening.

MELANIE:

That morning, about fifteen of my Georgia State college friends and I went rafting down the Chattahoochee River. A few of them lived at the Summit Creek apartment complex, so we ended up there just after lunch. After a while, some of them started doing wrestling moves and bodyslamming each other in the pool. They were showing off in front of Ted. I didn't think anything about it, because I never watched wrestling.

My friend used me to get Ted's autograph. As I was saying good-bye to one of my friends, I heard, "So, do you want my autograph?" I turned around, and as my friends were pleading to also get them one, I lightheartedly said, "Sure." He motioned me over to the apartment office to get me away from everyone. I thought he was an Atlanta Falcon football player. He gave me his autograph (I still have the autograph, which is framed in the house) and then asked me for my phone number, which I reluctantly gave him. I really did not intend to give it to him because he was so big. I am only five-four and he was not only a foot taller but also had a barrel chest. Although he was cute, he seemed so huge to me. But I gave it to him.

The next day we spent all day at the pool. We got to know each other and had a great time. In the early afternoon, I asked her out to dinner. After a fine meal, Melanie asked if I wanted to go out dancing. I accepted the invitation in order to spend more time with her. As we headed to the dance club, Melanie said, "Oh, by the way, Ted, be prepared. You will probably be the oldest person in the club."

"Come on, Melanie, I'm only twenty-six. I'm sure I won't be that much older than everyone."

And then it hit me. I had never asked Melanie her age. I was brought up that a man never asks a woman her age. So I asked, "Melanie, how old are you?"

"Nineteen."

"Nineteen? You look a lot older than that, and I mean that as a compliment." We had a great evening and Melanie was right, I was the oldest guy in the club.

MELANIE:

Ted was very charming and nice. I ended up breaking a date to go out with him. We had dinner at Benihana on Peachtree Street in downtown Atlanta. Afterward, we went to a disco called Pogo's and had a great time. Ted couldn't dance, but I still enjoyed his company.

Although there was an age difference, it was never really an issue. He was very sweet and treated me with class.

Melanie and I fell in love over the next four months. We spent every spare moment with each other. We were very compatible. She had morals, ethics, values, and was exactly what I always envisioned in a woman (and she was smokin' hot). When my grandmother came to Atlanta for a visit, we all went out and had a wonderful time. My grandmother really liked Melanie and her opinion spoke volumes. Deep down I knew Melanie was my soul mate.

In August, the Mid-South promotion started pressuring me to return. Bill Watts, and others, knew I was unhappy in Georgia. The heat between Jim and me ended, but I still wasn't getting the push to become NWA Heavyweight Champion. Melanie and I discussed all our options and we made a decision: our relationship could work long-distance. With mixed feelings, I left Georgia in August of 1981 and returned to the Mid-South territory. I

Just after Melanie and I were married.

rented an apartment in Baton Rouge at the same complex I was living in before. Melanie flew out with me and even helped organize and decorate my apartment.

After two weeks of being apart, we missed each other terribly. I was miserable without her. In late August, I called Melanie and said, "I need for you to come back down here to be with me." Neither of us was comfortable with the idea of living together outside of marriage, but I was overjoyed when she said, "Okay!" The same happiness wasn't shared by her parents, though. A few months later, on December 31, 1981, Melanie and I married. It was a small ceremony. The Junkyard Dog was my best man and my four-year-old son, Michael, was also a part of the service.

MELANIE:

At nineteen years old, I was in love. I was miserable without Ted and I would cry and cry. I finally moved to Baton Rouge. We were initially just going to live together, because Ted didn't want to pull me in right away because of his hectic road schedule. But being away from him was the hardest thing I had ever done. When you meet the person you are going to marry, you just know it. And I knew I was going to marry Ted.

At that point, I was still wrestling as a babyface. Sylvester Ritter, better known as the Junkyard Dog, and I were best friends. We lived near each other in Baton Rouge and traveled together throughout the territory. He was an excellent football player and had even played with the Green Bay Packers. He wasn't a great wrestler but he was a premier entertainer. Because he couldn't do a whole lot in the ring, his matches didn't last too long. I used to tease him that I would wrestle an hour every night, getting paid peanuts, and he'd walk into the ring, shake his butt to the crowd, howl at the moon, work five minutes, and he was the highest-paid guy in the territory. He would just laugh. JYD and I had many wonderful times together.

In Alexandria, Dick Murdoch and I were in a tag match against Ken Patera and Buck Robley. The crowd was hot, and you could tell by the way fans were throwing stuff into the ring that security was mediocre at best. The match ended in a Mexican standoff. As Dick and I were heading to the back, Patera grabbed a chair. Sensing total chaos, Dick screamed, "Don't do it, you idiot!" Patera looked at the crowd and threw the chair at us. Murdoch yelled to me, "Grab a chair and put it over your head!" Sure enough, Dick and I got nailed with an avalanche of chairs being thrown at us from the fans.

I wrestled a few matches against Paul Orndorff. Paul was a standout football player at the University of Tampa and was drafted by the Bears. He worked for every major wrestling promotion in the country and is probably one of the greatest wrestlers in the history of our business. In 2005, he was inducted into the WWE Hall of Fame.

One night in Jackson, Mississippi, Bill came up to Paul and me. "I am booking you guys in a babyface match."

Paul and I said, "No problem."

Bill then added, "And I want you guys to go for one hour—a draw." Heels usually call the match, but with both of us being babyfaces, we weren't used to calling a match. Doing it for an hour would be a challenge. "Look, I know you can do it. But if you guys feel like you can't go any more, I'll give you your finish."

Paul and I went out and had a great match. It was one of those nights that my confidence was taken to another level. We both called the match and I did things in the ring that I had never done before. Bill challenged both of us, and we rose to the challenge.

I was now making about fifteen hundred a week, but the long trips in the Mid-South territory hadn't changed one bit. With a pregnant wife at home, I was seeing less and less of her. I begged Bill Watts for some time off, but to no avail. He simply replied, "I can give you a day off here and there, but it is the nature of the beast. This is the wrestling business." Bill was a slave driver and pushed everyone to the limit. He was a brilliant promoter and booker, but the business was always first, family second.

One day I left my house to work a spot show in Hope, Arkansas. It was about a six-hour drive. I was genuinely upset about going to a show that was of little significance. For the past year, I worked like a slave and didn't have any time off. I really wanted to be home with Melanie. About forty miles out, I pulled into a convenience store. I called the Mid-South office and spoke to Bill Watts's secretary, Georgiana. "I have car trouble. They are going to have to tow my car back to Baton Rouge. I don't think I am going to make the show."

"Okay, when you get back to Baton Rouge, call Bill."

I hung up and called Melanie. "Hey, Melanie, guess what? Since Bill doesn't want to give me a day off, I just took one." I rehashed the lie I had told Georgiana and told Melanie to pull some steaks out of the freezer. We were finally going to enjoy a day together.

Once I got back to the house, I spent about an hour or so enjoying some quality time with Melanie. She had stopped traveling with me because of her pregnancy. Then I called Bill. One of his sons, Erik, answered the phone. "Hey, Erik, it's Ted. I had some car trouble and finally made it back home to Baton Rouge. Georgiana told me to call your dad. Is he there?"

"Okay. Hold on, Ted. Dad just now put the steaks on the grill." I wanted to take the phone and smash it against the wall. There I was busting my tail, driving all over the place trying to make a living. I couldn't even get a day off to spend with my wife, but Bill was sitting at home with his family having a barbecue.

Bill got on the phone and I explained to him my car trouble. He reiterated that I was in the main event for that night's show and that I really needed to be in Hope. Our brief chat ended with him telling me to call him back in fifteen minutes. Something inside me was telling me that my plan wasn't going to work.

When I called Bill back, he answered the phone and said, "Take a taxi to the airport. I've chartered a private plane to fly you to Hope." I couldn't believe it. The first and only time in the wrestling business I tried to miss a show, it didn't work.

A major phenomenon was happening in the world of professional wrestling. Vince McMahon Jr. took over World Wrestling Federation. He was starting to pull talent from around the country. Mid-South was affected, especially when the Wild Samoans—Afa and Sika—left. We also lost other heel talents. Bill Watts and Ernie Ladd were looking for a good heel to battle me and JYD. Ernie was the booker and categorically a great athlete. Standing almost seven feet tall and weighing more than three hundred pounds, Ernie was a heck of a worker and an overall great guy. He also served as one of my mentors. Ernie kept reminding me to look around the country to find a good heel to join the company.

One night after a show in Shreveport, I went to visit Ernie at his hotel room at the Sheraton. We chitchatted and then I told him that I had found the perfect heel. His eyes lit up and he wanted to know the name of the wrestler. In an excited manner I said, "Ernie, you are looking at him!" Ernie smiled and his eyes got as big as pumpkins. He started shaking his finger at me and said, "Why didn't I think of that? That's it!"

"Who would ever think that I would turn on JYD?" He shared it with Bill, who thought it was just the thing we needed.

The story line for me to turn heel was perfect. The wrestling fans had watched me wrestle as a good guy over the years. They knew JYD and I were close friends and that he was the best man at my wedding. I was always there to help him, like the time he was blinded in a match against the Freebirds. In and out of the ring, we were inseparable.

But I started to get a feeling in my stomach that maybe I shouldn't turn heel. I was getting cold feet. Ever since I had started in the business, I had always wrestled as a babyface. I wondered if I was making the right decision. I talked to JYD about it. He loved the idea and encouraged me, as did Ernie. He told me that I was a leader and helped me build my confidence.

To build the angle, Bill decided to have a drawing to see who would be the next wrestler to get a shot at my North American heavyweight title. JYD's name was drawn. JYD and I were both interviewed on television. We discussed our friendship and how the match for my title wasn't going to change our relationship. JYD stressed that it was nothing personal, but business was business and he was going to try his best to beat me. The match was going to take place on television in a few weeks.

In an effort to build interest, I unexpectedly "broke" my hand in a tag match with JYD against the Freebirds. To protect it, I started to wear a black glove on my right hand. I continued to wrestle with the glove and the announcers, Boyd Pierce and Bill Watts, made sure the fans knew that it still hadn't fully healed.

It was time for my match against JYD for the title. We had a clean, nip-and-tuck match. Near the end of the match, I went for my finishing move, the figure-four leglock. As I stepped over, JYD pushed me off with his legs; I went flying over the top rope and landed on the concrete floor. The referee began the ten-count. JYD stopped the referee from counting me out, and he went out to the floor to check on me and rolled me back into the ring. As he climbed back into the ring, I seized the moment and reached into my trunks. I inserted a foreign object in the glove. When JYD reached down to pick me up, I nailed him right in the jaw, knocking him out cold. I then covered him for the pin. The crowd was stunned. I had just screwed my best friend. It was the beginning of one of the hottest feuds in the history of the Mid-South territory. I was making more money than ever before.

JYD was the most popular wrestler in the territory. His character and personality appealed to both black and white fans. He was so popular among the fans that when a poll was taken by the New Orleans public school system to find out which sports figure the students would most want to come visit their school, JYD came in first, with players for the New Orleans Saints placing a distant second. When I wrestled JYD in New Orleans, they co-opted the football theme and chanted continuously, "Who dat? Who dat? Who dat say they gonna beat that Dog!"

For weeks, JYD always destroyed me in the match, but I would by hook or by crook cheat in the end to get the win. The fans were livid. Because of my feud with JYD, I had to be very careful. I was getting booed like never before and people literally wanted to kill me. Back then lots of people took wrestling seriously. Bill knew about my concerns, so he beefed up security. The first time I wrestled JYD in New Orleans, I told Grizzly Smith that there was no way I was going to drive my own car to the arena. I knew the fans would destroy it. Grizzly agreed and drove me to the show. Unfortunately for Grizzly, on the first night the fans punctured all four of his tires because he had brought me to the show. Poor Grizzly, it seemed like I was always doing damage to his cars.

I was now the leader of the Rat Pack. We even had a manager, Skandor Akbar. The Rat Pack was a heel group that included "Hacksaw" Jim Duggan, Matt Borne, and me. King Kong Bundy and Mr. Olympia later joined the group. We wreaked havoc across the territory.

JIM DUGGAN:

When I arrived in the Mid-South territory, Teddy was one of the top heels in the promotion. I came in from Texas All-Star Wrestling in San Antonio. Bill Watts put me together with Matt Borne and Teddy and we worked as the Rat Pack. We were a pretty good heel team. Teddy had the loaded glove and could always draw heat with it against the babyface. We did a lot of three-man tag matches with the Freebirds.

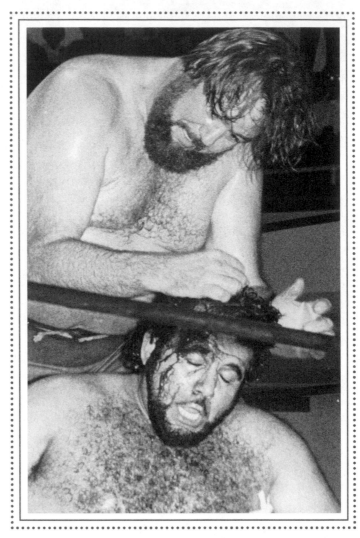

Skandor Akbar and Grizzly Smith.

Though we didn't last too long together, we had some great battles
with the Junkyard Dog and Mr. Olympia.

I started always wearing a black glove. The glove was part of my gimmick to
help me secure a record number of wins. One night in a grueling match
against Mr. Wrestling II in Tulsa, he started to get the better of me. After nail-
ing me with his trademark high running knee lift, he thought he was about to

put me in his finisher. Skandor Akbar threw me a foreign object when the referee's and Mr. Wrestling II's backs were turned. I loaded the glove with the foreign object and popped him in the head, knocking him out. I covered my unconscious opponent and attained the victory. The fans were angry.

As we left the ring, a big, farm-fed guy blocked our path to the dressing room. Now, in the wrestling business, you never look for trouble with the fans. But if trouble starts, you finish it. If a fan ever gets you in a situation where you must fight him, then you'd better come out victorious. If not, you'd be fired on the spot.

The guy wouldn't let me pass. Initially, I was going to just step around him, but he kept moving in front of me. He hit me. Immediately, I got in his face and put my finger right between his eyes and said, "Don't you ever touch me again!" As I turned and walked away, I was shoved in the back. I turned around and with all my might punched the guy right in the face. He went down like a tree, and then he started to get back up. I kicked him as hard as I could right in the face. Blood was everywhere. By then, the police had showed up and he was carted away. At the same time, all the wrestlers from the back had come out to help me. When I got back to the dressing room, I noticed a lump in the black glove. I had broken my hand. It wasn't my first injury and it wouldn't be my last.

JIM DUGGAN:

One night in Oklahoma City, we were wrestling in a rodeo arena. They had just had a rodeo event the night before. To make room for the ring, they simply moved all the dirt to one side and into this giant mound. Since everything was wide open, Bill Watts wouldn't spring for security. All the heels had to stay around to watch each other's back. At that time, it was dangerous to be a heel, and it was pretty common to have fights with the fans and even riots, especially in Louisiana.

In the main event, Teddy was in a hot finish with Mr. Wrestling II. As all the heels sat up in the bleachers, high enough to

see over the big dirt mound, Teddy loaded his glove and knocked out
Mr. Wrestling II. The place just went crazy. Liquored up, many of the
fans started attacking Teddy. All the heels jumped up and started
heading down to the bleachers to help him. But the first one heading
down the stairs was King Kong Bundy. Since he was so big, he was
moving slowly, one step at a time. We screamed at Bundy to hurry up
as Teddy was fighting off the fans one by one. We eventually got
Teddy back safely to the locker room.

I have a cauliflower ear. In the wrestling business, just about everyone does.
From headlocks to getting punched, the outer ear takes a major pounding.
After a period of time, blood and fluid builds up in the ear. If it isn't drained,
the outer ear will remain permanently swollen and deformed, and it looks like
a piece of cauliflower—hence the name. The first time my ear started to swell,
I was in some serious pain. I didn't know what to do. Fortunately, or so I
thought, Jack and Jerry Brisco said they had cauliflower ear and knew exactly
how to treat it.

The first thing they did was ice my ear down, numbing it real good.
They then stuck a needle in the swollen part of the ear and drained out all the
blood and fluid. My ear felt better. But the next night, my ear hurt even more
and it was much larger than before. Jack and Jerry once again drained my ear.
The next day my ear was even bigger. What I later found out was that after
draining the ear, it had to be packed with gauze. If not, a cauliflower ear would
just get bigger and bigger! My two friends had just given me a very painful rib.

That weekend, I had to go to St. Louis for a TV match. When I got
there, I told the jobber that I would call the match and not to worry. I was
going to make sure he got his spots but asked him to please make sure he
didn't touch my left ear. I reiterated it and even pointed and showed him my
swollen ear. He agreed. After starting the match, the first thing the kid did
after we locked up was give me a forearm to my left ear. The pain was unbearable. It also made me mad. I immediately shot on him and beat the living
tar out of the kid. The match was over in about three minutes. The next day I
flew back to Atlanta and went straight to see my physician. He drained my ear

and packed it tightly with gauze. To keep everything in place and maintain pressure on my ear, he wrapped my head. I looked like one of those characters in the painting *The Spirit of '76*.

Although Melanie was very mature for her age, I was still concerned about her being alone and pregnant. While on the road, I would call her four or five times a day—oh, how I wish we had cell phones back in the day. One evening after my match in Lake Charles, I telephoned Melanie to check in. She wasn't feeling well and wanted me to immediately come home. I grabbed my gear and headed out of the arena. As I pulled out of the parking lot, I ran into my friend Chuck. He was a Louisiana highway patrolman. I told him that I thought Melanie was going into delivery any minute. He said, "Ted, don't worry. I will send out a message giving you a green light all the way to Baton Rouge." I did that hundred-and-forty-mile drive in about an hour and a half! A few days later, November 8, 1982, Teddy Jr. was born in Baton Rouge.

With a new infant at home, I finally decided that it was time to once again leave the grueling Mid-South territory. I told Bill there was more to life than money. I had been through one divorce, and I was making my family a priority. Bill couldn't believe it. "But Ted, you are leaving so much money on the table." I thanked Bill, and after I lost a Loser Leaves Town match, I headed back to the Georgia territory.

I went back to Georgia because the trips were shorter and I was able to be home almost every night. I didn't make as much money, but at least I was home with my family. Georgia was also where Melanie was raised. She had lots of friends and family in the area and there would be someone there for her when I was on the road.

MELANIE:

We moved to my parents' home in Clarkston, Georgia, because Ted could work in a territory where he could be home almost every night. Plus, I was homesick. I missed many of my friends. After a few weeks in Georgia, it quickly dawned on me that all my old friends were single and they lived a different lifestyle. As a new mother and wife, I had other priorities. My parents had moved back to Mississippi a few months prior to Ted and me relocating. After a year or so, to be closer to my parents, we decided to move to Clinton, Mississippi.

In Georgia, I initially wrestled as a babyface. Tommy Rich and I had started teaming again. I then turned heel and feuded with Tommy. We ran an angle similar to what JYD and I had done in the Mid-South territory. After I beat JYD in a Loser Leaves Town match, he went back under a mask and called himself Stagger Lee. Everyone knew it was JYD, but I could never get the ref to see it. Then, after I beat Tommy in a Loser Leaves Town match, Tommy went back under a mask and called himself Mister R.

BILL WATTS:

What made Teddy so important to me was that he wasn't selfish in the ring. No matter who he was working with, Ted would make sure it was an excellent match. He would always make the match the top priority, not him. He would get the match over, rather than just getting himself over. That was huge because many guys were selfish. Getting them over was more important to them than the match. Ted had that special something that if he was in the match, no matter what, he would make the match work.

That Christmas, I invited my mother to come spend the holidays with us. She agreed and the entire family went to the airport to pick her up. As she exited the jetway, she looked so frail. Mom reeked of alcohol and cigarette smoke. Still, I was so happy to see her. She had a blast with her grandson, Teddy. After a few days, however, she became quite ill. We rushed her to the emergency room at Piedmont Hospital in Atlanta. After she had her vitals checked, Mom was hospitalized. The doctors told us she had bronchitis, emphysema, and other problems that were related to her excessive drinking and smoking. She was dying.

MELANIE:

When my mother-in-law got off the plane in Atlanta, you could hear the alcohol bottles jingling in her purse. She was told not to drink or smoke; she was doing both. A few days later, we had to rush Helen to the emergency room. She had got so bad that Ted's grandmother was flown in to be by her side. I took her to the hospital twice a day. While in ICU, I will never forget watching Ted's grandmother praying for her daughter. For weeks, she sat at the end of Helen's bed every night just praying for her.

Helen was eventually put on a ventilator. She was in very bad health because of her drinking. Her pancreas had swelled and she had caught pneumonia. Her kidneys soon shut down and she then passed away.

Mom remained in the hospital for nearly two weeks. My grandmother flew into town and stayed with us. Melanie brought my grandmother and Teddy to the hospital twice a day. My grandmother cried and prayed, hoping my mom would recover. But it was too much for her to overcome. She died on March 4, 1984. As I entered my fourth decade of life, both my father and mother were now dead. With my two brothers at my side we buried her in Willcox.

Because of all that had happened in my personal life and the Atlanta business being down, Melanie and I decided to move back to the Mid-South. Jim Duggan had called me and said that Bill wanted me to return. I returned in October of 1984 for my final run in Mid-South, which lasted through the summer of 1987. We moved near Melanie's parents in Clinton. It was a perfect move for both my career and my marriage.

BILL WATTS:

Teddy always tried to better himself and learn more. By going from territory to territory, he learned from a lot of different people. That is why Teddy was such a great wrestler. To me, the true measure of a Superstar is that they get over everywhere they work. And Ted got over everywhere he worked.

I continued to wrestle as a heel and had started a grudge with "Hacksaw" Jim Duggan. In early 1985 we entered into a very hot angle coined the Best Dressed Man in the South feud. We had a contest to see who the fans thought looked better in a tuxedo. I cut promo after promo where I degraded Jim by calling him, among other things, a slob. When it came to the actual show-down on TV, I lost the contest.

The fans overwhelmingly cheered for Duggan. I didn't agree with the results. So with the cameras following me, I headed out to the parking lot to argue with the guys in the TV truck. After degrading all of them, I headed back to the arena. But out of the corner of my eye, I saw Jim's car. I took the baseball bat that I had been carrying to protect myself and smashed the wind-shield. My intention was to smash only the windshield. But for whatever rea-son, it didn't shatter the way I expected. So I began to smash the headlights and windows. The cameras were rolling the entire time and it made great TV.

JIM DUGGAN:

I probably worked with Teddy more than any other guy in the business. We wrestled in Georgia, Mid-South, and even World Wrestling Federation. In March of 1988, Teddy and I wrestled against each other at *WrestleMania IV* in Atlantic City. Virgil and Andre the Giant were in his corner. After Andre interfered—breaking a few of my ribs with his big hand—Teddy stole the win from me at *WrestleMania*.

In one of my favorite interviews that I used to give, I'd rib Teddy, saying, "DiBiase may be the greatest technical wrestler in the sport today, but he can't fight a lick."

In all seriousness, Teddy is a true friend and was a great wrestler. As a second-generation wrestler, he was very polished in the ring. He was a good-looking young guy and worked very hard in the ring.

"Hacksaw" Jim Duggan is one of my good friends. Along with "Dr. Death" Steve Williams, he was one of the strongest men in the business. He wasn't a great technical wrestler, but he had energy, personality, and character, which made him one of the best workers in the history of our business. Jim and I were good friends and we shared lots of good times on the road. We also had some great matches. I will never forget our angle in Tulsa.

Jim is a man's man and strong as a bull. But I never met anyone so afraid to blade. For a period of weeks working the Best Dressed Man angle, Jim kept guzzling me. Not only would he not sell for me, but he wouldn't draw color. Bill Watts and I finally smartened him up. In the next match, I told Jim that I was going to throw him into the ringpost and that he should blade when he hit. Jim hit the post, and there was hardly any color. I told him to do it again. That pattern repeated for what seemed like five minutes. Finally Jim asked, "Hey, what's going on?" I just laughed.

Jim and I wrestled in what I call the mother of all gimmick matches. It was a Loser Leaves Town match, inside a ten-foot steel cage, with us dressed in tuxedos and a loaded coal miner's glove attached to a twelve-foot pole. Back then, there was no Internet to advertise the results of a show. We ran the match throughout the entire territory, starting at the Superdome in New Orleans. About twenty thousand fans witnessed Jim Duggan beat me. After that, I wasn't able to return to Bourbon Street for about three months.

Later, I teamed with Steve "Dr. Death" Williams. Bill Watts thought it would be good if I took Doc under my wing. We became a heck of a tag team. We worked with every tag team in the territory, including Hector and Chavo Guerrero and the Rock 'n' Roll Express. In fact, in 1985 we were voted the

Tag Team of the Year by *Pro Wrestling Illustrated*. We had good chemistry. He always wanted to learn in order to get better. He was probably the strongest guy I had ever been with in the wrestling ring, other than Andre the Giant. He was naturally strong and I really don't think he knew his own strength.

Doc was an All-American in both football and wrestling at the University of Oklahoma. He went on to work in every major wrestling promotion in the United States, as well as New Japan and All-Japan. Even though he was a Sooner, and I'm a huge Cornhusker fan, we were the best of friends.

One Saturday afternoon, Doc took me to an OU game. We had a great time and I met a lot of the coaches and players. After the game, we had to leave Norman for the evening matches in Tulsa. It was about a one-hundred-twenty-five-mile drive and the traffic was at a standstill. Doc had a van and it was loaded with beer. After not moving for about ten minutes, Doc looked over at me with this childish grin. He then floored it and headed down a one-way road that had been blocked off for traffic control. A university police officer blew his whistle for us to stop. He even hit the side of the van with his hand. But what could he do? There were way too many people and there was too much going on.

About fifteen miles down the road, two guys in a sports car were preventing Doc from passing on the two-lane highway. As Doc tried to go around them, they sped up, preventing us from passing. This continued for about ten minutes, pissing both of us off. We could see the guys' facial expressions. They thought it was funny. They weren't about to let two guys in a van pass them. Doc finally took an opportunity and passed them on the median. With that childish grin that only Doc has, he looked over at me and said, "Put your seat belt on, I am going to teach these guys a lesson. They'll either stop or smash the rear of my van." Doc slammed on the brakes and the guys stopped just inches from the van. We both pulled over and they got out like they were going to kick our butts. Then Doc and I got out of the van, and the two nerds quickly ran back into their car and locked the doors. Doc began cursing them out. I just stood on the passenger's side with my arms crossed. They sat there scared to death. Right as we were walking away, Doc slammed his arms on the roof of their car, leaving an indentation shaped like a birdbath. The guys never said a word.

To this day, Doc and I speak on a regular basis. He is a born-again Christian. I hope that I had some influence on him changing his life for the better. He is also a throat cancer survivor, and he attributes his survival to the grace of God. He has a hole in his throat and relies on a stoma—a surgically created opening in his throat that allows him to speak. Doc is committed to giving his testimony to people from the wrestling ring.

"DR. DEATH" STEVE WILLIAMS:

When Ted came back into the territory, Bill told me to watch him real closely. I was to study how he conducted himself as a professional both in and outside the ring. Bill was right. Ted was not only one of the classiest guys I had ever met, but he was one of the best ring technicians. Ted taught me so much about the wrestling business and life in general.

We had many great times on the road, from the football games to racing throughout the territory in our new Nissan 300ZXs. Ted became a close friend. Even to this day, we remain the best of friends. He was a big influence on me with respect to my salvation and I deeply appreciate everything that Ted has done for me.

In late 1985, Ric Flair came to the territory to defend the NWA world heavyweight title. I was given the opportunity of a lifetime to go against Ric for the title. Prior to the start of the match, with Ric and me both in the ring, Dick Murdoch came to the ring. He was still one of the most hated wrestlers around. On TV, he got on the microphone and said, "Look, Teddy. You and I go way back. You aren't ready for this match. Tonight is my night. So just step aside."

"Look, Dick, nothing personal. But there is no way that I am going to pass up this opportunity." Dick responded by hitting me square in the face and tossed me outside the ring. He threw me into the steel ringpost and busted me open.

I came into the ring with a bandaged and bloody head. I wouldn't be

Taking on Ric Flair for the NWA title.

deterred from my title shot. The fans saw this as a heroic effort and cheered me on. Flair and I wrestled for what seemed like an hour. It was a great match, and Flair was a tremendous worker. As I set up Flair for the figure-four, he kicked me off; I took a bump over the top rope and landed on the outside concrete floor. Dick came back down to ringside to help me, but he quickly changed his mind and gave me a Brain Buster on the concrete floor. I was counted out and Flair retained his title. The injury allowed me four weeks of work in Japan. When I returned, I fought Dick throughout the territory and I became one of the most popular wrestlers in Mid-South.

TERRY TAYLOR:

Bill Watts was not afraid to work his talent to death—sometimes three times a day. One New Year's Eve, we worked in the afternoon and early evening, and did a late-night show that was to end right before midnight. There was also a big New Year's Eve party scheduled afterward at the show for everybody who paid to watch the wrestling event. There was a live band, food, drinks, et cetera. The show ended about eleven-thirty.

As the clock approached midnight, the band called all the wrestlers back into the ring. We were all dancing, drinking, singing, and having a great time bringing in the New Year. After a while, Teddy said, "I'm going to the bathroom and then grab a bite to eat."

I asked, "What room are you in?"

He said, "Twelve forty-one, why?"

"Nothing, maybe I will come up later."

So Teddy heads to the bathroom. I am still in the ring, singing with the band. The band decided to take a ten-minute break. So I got on the microphone and said to the crowd, "Do you guys want this party to end?"

"No!"

"You want to stay up all night and party?"

"Yeah!"

"Well, in room 1241, I have two kegs of beer and everybody is invited!" About a half hour later, the party ended.

Teddy and I took the elevator up to the twelfth floor. I got out first to see if anybody went up; there was a line all the way from the elevator, down the hallway, and back over to room 1241. Teddy asked, "What are all these people doing here?"

I coyly replied, "I don't know." When Teddy went to get in his room, the people tried to go in with him. They thought he was kidding when he said there was no beer in the room.

During my three-year stint with Mid-South, I was making wrestling trips to and from Japan. I was probably going to Japan two or three times a year. I was making a name for myself overseas and Giant Baba really took care of me. I was also getting a major push. Bruiser Brody and Stan Hansen were the hottest tag team in All-Japan. Stan was also the most popular foreign wrestler in all of Japan. Bruiser decided to work for a rival promotion, New Japan. It created an opening, so Stan asked me to be his partner. It was a privilege for Stan to ask me, and of course, I agreed to work with him.

Mid-South started to change. In an effort to compete with World Wrestling Federation, Bill Watts officially changed the name of the Mid-South promotion to the Universal Wrestling Federation. Although business was doing well, it wasn't doing as well as World Wrestling Federation. Vince McMahon had transformed the wrestling industry. He made many changes geared to attract a family audience: making wrestling less violent, taking away the blood and gore, and introducing more cartoonlike wrestling characters. Unfortunately, Bill had started too late and didn't have the financial support to compete with Vince. He later sold the company to Jim Crockett Promotions.

Vince had been recruiting talent from the various territories. I initially felt that Vince was destroying the sport by the way he cherry-picked talent. And Vince had the audacity to run his shows in our territory. But deep down, I knew that he was a marketing mastermind and that the wrestling landscape was changing. Vince had created *WrestleMania*—wrestling's Super Bowl— and with 93,000 people in attendance for *WrestleMania III,* I knew it was only a matter of time before the territorial system would dissipate. Guys like Terry Funk had predicted it years ago. So when Paul Orndorff, Jim Duggan, and the Junkyard Dog left to go to New York, I sensed that maybe it was time for me to get on board.

12
THE MILLION DOLLAR MAN

A few days after I started wrestling in Japan, the folks at the All-Japan office told me that Bruce Prichard had called me a few times and that I needed to contact him as soon as possible. Once I made contact, Bruce said, "Ted, whatever you do, please don't sign a contract with Crockett until you have a chance to talk to Vince McMahon. He is more than interested in you." I took Bruce's advice and told him that I wouldn't do anything until the tour was over in about three weeks.

I got home from Japan in early May of 1987. I kept waiting for the phone to ring. About four days went by and I hadn't heard a word from anyone. I started thinking that maybe the deal with World Wrestling Federation had fallen through. I was outside on the deck, thinking, when Melanie told me that Vince McMahon was on the phone. I was excited as I got on the phone with him. After we exchanged pleasantries, he said, "Ted, I am very interested in you coming to work for World Wrestling Federation. As a matter of fact, we have an idea for a new character. You and I both know that everything has been done and redone in wrestling. But this is something that is original and has never been done before. We think you fit the bill for the job."

"That's great, but what is it?"

"No, no. I'm not going to tell you over the phone. I want you to fly up here and we will talk face-to-face. I'll have a prepaid ticket waiting for you at the Jackson airport and there will be a limousine waiting for you at the airport in New York." The next thing I knew, I was flying first-class to New York. I was then chauffeured in a stretch limousine to the World Wrestling Federation headquarters in Stamford.

The limo pulled into the headquarters' parking lot. By the look of the building, I knew that the company was very successful. As I walked in, I noticed how perfectly decorated it was, and all the staff treated me with the utmost professionalism. I was taken to Vince's office, where I was met by Vince and Pat Patterson. Pat was Vince's right-hand man. He was a great wrestler and had been in the business for years. He knew what he was doing, which is why he was Vince's top consultant. I had known Pat from my first run in World Wrestling Federation, and we got along real well.

For an hour, Vince told me about his vision for the future of professional wrestling. Then Vince said he had this idea for an unprecedented character and he wanted me to be the talent for it. He praised my wrestling skills and ability to speak on the microphone. He also believed that the manner in which I conducted myself outside the ring was an added bonus. "I am completely convinced that you would be perfect for the role."

"Great! What is this new character?"

"I can't tell you what it is until you say yes and sign with us," Vince said. "Until you agree, I am not going to take the chance of giving away a great idea and have it show up somewhere else."

I told Vince that I appreciated him flying me up there and I was about 90 percent sure that I was on board. I just needed some time to talk it over with my wife. He understood.

Vince had to leave to take an important phone call. Pat Patterson then looked at me and said, "Ted, let me tell you this. This isn't just an idea that somebody came up with. This is Vince's idea. If Vince was going to put the tights on and become a wrestler, this is the character that he would be. So, all I want you to know is that because it is *his* idea, he is going to do everything he can to make sure it gets over." I trusted Pat, so I knew this was a great opportunity.

PAT PATTERSON:

During some downtime, I was alone with Teddy. I said, "For Christ sake, Teddy, you have to take that opportunity. I don't know what this new character could be. But if it is Vince's baby, then you know he is going to go all the way with it. He is going to do whatever it takes to make it work."

When Vince came back in, he asked me how much money Crockett had offered me. I told him the truth. Vince honestly said, "Ted, I am not going to promise you a specific dollar amount. But I can promise that you will make more money than you have ever made in your life."

When I got back home, I told Melanie about the offer. Immediately, I called my mentor, Terry Funk. Terry was not only an amazing talent but he had a clear understanding of the future of professional wrestling. I remembered him telling me back in college that there would come a time in the business when wrestlers would travel the world and perform in front of large crowds just like rock stars. So I told him about Vince's offer.

TERRY FUNK:

I told Teddy, "If Vince McMahon has an idea, pack your bags, go to New York City, and don't look back." It was the right time for him to make the move. I knew where the business was heading (and still do), and believe me, wrestling was changing. There were approximately thirty-six to thirty-nine territorial promotions. Although Bill Watts was doing well, it was only a matter of time before World Wrestling Federation would dominate the sport. Vince had the energy and the money, and was in the right geographical location. And now with national television, it spelled the end for the regional promotions.

A couple of days later I called Vince. "Vince, I've had some time to think about the offer and even ran it by a couple of people whom I respect and trust. I want to let you know that I am your guy and I am coming to work for you in World Wrestling Federation!"

"That is great."

"So now can you tell me the idea?" I asked.

Vince chuckled. "No, I don't want to talk to you about it over the phone. I will send two first-class plane tickets in the mail for you and your wife. I want you to spend the weekend in New York."

After I hung up with Vince, I immediately called Jim Crockett. I never really liked Jim. It goes back to when I wrestled for Sam Muchnick in St. Louis and Jim was there watching. He was arrogant and had this aura about him. It seemed that just because he was this big-time promoter, everybody had to kiss his butt. It made my call to him all the sweeter. "Jim, I have some bad news for you. I am not signing the deal. I have accepted an offer to work for Vince McMahon. He made me an offer that I couldn't refuse and I think it is going to be the biggest break in my career. I'm sorry it didn't work out."

BOB GEIGEL:

At the time, I didn't think Ted's move to World Wrestling Federation was the right one. I wasn't too fond of Vince McMahon Jr. I didn't approve of what he was doing to the territories. However, now, as time has gone by, it is apparent that Vince has done a tremendous job in taking over wrestling. The guys he took from the various territories became stars. I turned out to be wrong.

A few days later, Melanie and I were off to New York. It was a good break for Melanie. My in-laws took care of Teddy. When we arrived, a stretch limousine was waiting to take us to meet with Vince in Stamford. Once we arrived, Melanie was introduced to everyone, and I went into Vince's office to meet with him and Pat. Ironically, Melanie was entertained in the outer office by none other than Jim Barnett. Jim had sold his interests in the Georgia territory and left Atlanta to work for Vince McMahon.

I signed a two-year continuing contract. Every two years the contract would roll over unless I decided to opt out by giving written notice within ninety days of its expiration. Vince then laid out his entire idea and described the new character. "Ted, this character is a filthy-rich heel and we are going to make people believe that you are really rich. He is so rich that he throws his money around like it is nothing. He can buy anyone and anything. His god is money and he will live by the motto 'Every man has his price.' " I started smiling like a Cheshire cat.

"Ted, you will travel all over the country first-class. There will be a limousine to take you to and from the hotel, the show, and anywhere else you want to go. I will always make sure you have a wad of hundreds on you and you will never have to worry about a penny. We'll also find you your very own personal bodyguard and valet." I couldn't believe it. The character seemed too good to be true. "And Ted, you're going to be the hottest and most hated heel in all of professional wrestling." I agreed.

"The only thing that I don't have nailed down yet is the name."

Without hesitation I said, "I know what we should call him—how about the Million Dollar Man?"

Vince and Pat simultaneously said, "That's it," and the Million Dollar Man was born.

PAT PATTERSON:

Vince explained the character to Ted. It was the first time I ever heard the details. I thought the gimmick was great. Vince said that he never told anyone because he needed the right guy with a good head on his shoulders to work the gimmick. He told Teddy that he would always have to ride in limousines, live like a king, eat at fancy restaurants. I knew Teddy was the right person for the character.

The meeting ended with me getting some immediate on-the-job training. Vince treated me and my wife to an extravagant weekend in New York. We were escorted all over New York in his personal limousine and given the best room at the historic and pricey Helmsley Palace hotel in Manhattan. We dined at gourmet restaurants such as the Water Club, and had two orchestra seats to see the Broadway musical *Cats*.

The entire weekend, I asked Melanie to pinch me. I couldn't believe it was real. It was like a fairy tale. I remembered looking in the mirror of the hotel room and saying to Melanie, "I can't believe this is happening." I thought back to when I had started wrestling in 1975. For twelve years I had mastered my craft. I was a good wrestler. I had great ring psychology and spoke well on the microphone. Wrestling had become mainstream. I had paid my dues. All those years I wore out car after car, driving thousands upon thousands of miles. I stayed in cheap hotels, sleeping on box springs and sometimes even on the floor. I would eat as cheaply as possible, living primarily on bologna sandwiches. And now Vince was going to fly me first-class to every event. I was going to be chauffeured everywhere in a limousine and my valet would carry my bags. I would stay in upscale hotels and dine at five-star restaurants. I would never, ever have to worry about money. Not in my wildest dreams did I ever think I would get such an opportunity. It seemed too good to be true.

I didn't jump into the World Wrestling Federation ring to wrestle right away. I told Vince that I had existing obligations in All-Japan. And of course, he said that he expected that I would fulfill them. When I got to Japan, I told Giant Baba that I couldn't work for him anymore after the tour because of my new contract with World Wrestling Federation. Baba understood, wished me the best, and stressed that I was welcome back anytime.

I called Melanie from Japan. After some small talk she said, "Honey, I have some exciting news for you. I'm pregnant." For the third time in my life, I was going to be a father. I was so excited.

Before I ever wrestled a single match for World Wrestling Federation, the viewers were introduced to my character through a series of vignettes. They carefully created vignettes to make me as hated as possible. It was slapstick comedy at its best. The first one showed me in the back of a limousine counting my money. While I was counting the money, I got a paper cut. I told my driver and personal valet, Virgil, to take me to the hospital. When we got to the emergency room, I demanded to see a doctor. The attending nurse said I had to wait like everyone else. "Look, you don't understand. I am the Million Dollar Man. I don't wait on anybody." The nurse reiterated that I had to wait. All of a sudden I called Virgil with a snap of my fingers. He pulled out a wad of money and handed the nurse three or four hundred dollars. The nurse took the money and said, "I'll be right back." Sure enough, she came back with a doctor. I arrogantly replied, "That's what I thought." Then I turned to the camera and said, "Don't get upset with the nurse. She is no different than you. She did the same thing that anybody would do. She took the money. Just like her, everybody has a

Virgil and I.

price for the Million Dollar Man." And I then ended it with my deep, arrogant laugh. It became the standard punch line for all my early interviews.

There was another vignette where I went to a restaurant. We pulled up and there was a long line waiting to get in. With Virgil by my side, I walked right up to the front of the line. I told the maître d' that I needed a table for two.

"Sir, you are going to have to wait in line like everyone else."

"Look, you don't understand. I am the Million Dollar Man. I don't wait on anybody."

"I'm sorry, sir, but you are going to have to wait."

Out of the blue, I called Virgil with a snap of my fingers. He pulled out a wad of money and handed the maître d' four or five hundred dollars. The maître d' took the money and said, "Well, sir, I think we have a table for two."

One of the people in line started complaining and came up to me and said, "Hey, pal, who do you think you are?" I just looked at him and smiled. I then took a step back and Virgil stepped in with his great big arms and foul demeanor. The guy just backed down and slithered back in line. Virgil and I got seated at the table and we were waited on hand and foot. Then I turned to the camera and said, "Don't get upset with the maître d'. He is no different than you. He did the same thing that anybody would do. He took the money. Just like him, everybody has a price for the Million Dollar Man."

One more vignette had me go into an exclusive hotel. I asked the front-desk clerk what their best room was.

"The honeymoon suite."

"I'll take it."

"I'm sorry, sir, it's taken."

"Well, that is the room I want. That is the best room and I want it."

"I'm sorry, sir, it is taken and there is a couple in there right now." Again, I called Virgil with a snap of my fingers. He pulled out a wad of money and handed the clerk five or six hundred dollars. He accepted the money and the scene quickly changed to show him kicking the honeymoon couple out of the room. Then I turned to the camera and said, "Don't get upset with the front-desk guy. He is no different than you. He did the same thing that anybody would do. He took the money. Just like him, everybody has a price for the Million Dollar Man."

The vignettes were being aired and I hadn't yet been seen wrestling. When I finally made it to the live shows, the immediate response from the fans was that I was a pompous ass who thought he was God because he had lots of money. And that was the whole idea of the character. The vignettes laid down the foundation for people to hate me.

BOBBY "THE BRAIN" HEENAN:

Ted's Million Dollar Man gimmick was excellent. No one could have done it better than him, except Vince McMahon. He carried himself as a true professional. The funny thing is that most true professionals in wrestling aren't nice guys. Ted is a really nice guy. When I was producing interviews for WWE, I had to watch over the guys, monitor what they were saying, and keep up with them. But I never had to worry about Ted. He did everything on time, spoke proper English, and got right to the point with his interviews. He is a true professional.

After the airing of the introductory vignettes, I started wrestling. I wrestled jobbers on TV and easily squashed them. During the 1980s, unless you were shooting an angle, very rarely did you see competitive matches on free TV. Most of the televised matches were what we called enhancement matches, which were designed to highlight the stars. Today, you see top guys wrestling each other every week.

I continued my pompous antics by casually throwing money at people as I made my way back to the dressing room. While they scrambled to pick it up, I said, "That's it. Go down there like a bunch of pigs. Pick it up and wallow in it. Everybody has a price for the Million Dollar Man." I left, laughing in my arrogant and evil way. We realized we had made a mistake, because we used real hundred-dollar bills. We quickly found out that it was very difficult for people to hate me if I was throwing money at them.

We decided to no longer just throw money at the crowd; now I picked plants from the crowd and made them do humiliating things for money. For almost the entire first year that I wrestled, we did the insulting skits everywhere I wrestled. They took three or four hundred dollars right off the top of the house and they brought me the money. At the end of every one of my matches, I told the audience, "Okay, once again I am here to prove a point. And that point is that everybody has a price for the Million Dollar Man. Each and every one of you I can buy. It is only a question of how much." I would also make sure they would never win the money (off camera they would get paid).

When you combined the arrogance with me easily destroying my opponents on TV, I became the most hated heel in the company. I was a blowhard and had the muscle to back up my word. It was all part of the character.

For instance, I went on live TV and told the crowd that once again I was going to prove my point, and that was that anybody had a price. More specifically, everybody had a price for the Million Dollar Man. And to prove my point, I had Virgil give me five hundred dollars. "I have five hundred dollars here for somebody who's willing to bark like a dog." Virgil and I scrolled through the crowd and then I told Virgil to bring me the young lady I indicated. We brought her up and I said, "Look, I have five hundred dollars here if you can bark like a dog. But you have to do it right. Can you bark like a dog?"

"Yes."

"Okay, let me hear you bark!"

She went, "Woof, woof, woof."

"Wait, wait. Dogs don't stand up. They get down on all fours. Get down on your hands and knees and let me hear you bark like a dog." I was just humiliating her, but she barked. Once again, I interrupted, "Come on. You can do better than that. Let me hear the high-pitched bark of a Chihuahua." I continued to humiliate her until I finally looked at Virgil and said, "What do you think?" Virgil simply shook his head no and I added, "I don't think so either. Unfortunately, when you don't get the job done right, you don't get the money. Virgil, get her out of here." She left humiliated as the fans were booing. They literally wanted to hang me.

I did my thing and told the crowd that I could buy them. Virgil handed me the money and I said, "I have some money here for someone who is willing to kiss my stinky feet. I just wrestled some twenty minutes and I have been sweating in my socks and boots. I have three hundred dollars for anybody who will come up in the ring and kiss my dirty, smelly, rotten feet." And you would not believe how many people raised their hands. I spotted the plant and Virgil motioned him to the ring. I berated the kid for a while until he finally kissed my feet.

To my surprise, the same kid became a Superstar in WWE: Rob Van Dam. I never knew it until one day somebody told me. While I was working as a producer for WWE, I met Rob for the first time. I jokingly asked, "Hey, kid, do you want to kiss my feet for the second time?" He laughed and we had a good time visiting. His aerial moves are awesome and he is very over with the crowd.

The most talked about skit that I had ever done was with a little kid where I asked him to dribble a basketball fifteen times in a row. I get asked about that one skit more than all the others. I can't tell you how many people want to know about it. I guess it was because it was pretty amazing that this small, maybe six-year-old African-American kid could even dribble a ball. But we had rehearsed everything. It was all a setup but no one knew it. I kicked that ball away after the fourteenth dribble and berated him. The camera showed a close-up of the kid's big crocodile tears filling his eyes, and then he ran to his mother, who was at the edge of the platform, and jumped in her arms. Unreal. It was a perfect television moment.

The crowd went nuts. They believed the whole act. As I left for the dressing room, people were throwing things and saying some nasty stuff to me. They wanted to strangle me.

No matter where I went, Virgil was always by my side. It was Vince's idea to bring Virgil in as my valet. I didn't meet him until we put the final touches on the character. His name is Mike Jones and he's from Pittsburgh. Mike had some wrestling experience, but Vince hired him for his look. He had huge arms, a bald head, and a great physique. Vince laid out to Virgil exactly what he was going to do. He was going to carry my bags and chauffeur me. He would open the car door and my hotel door. Virgil was my muscle and manager at ringside. He was my personal servant everywhere we went in public. That was his job and he got paid well to do it. Virgil never took the role personally.

The name Virgil evolved from a meeting over dinner. After I signed with World Wrestling Federation, Pat Patterson, Bobby Heenan, and I went out to eat. Over steaks, Pat said, "Guys, we have to think of a name for Ted's servant." After throwing out stupid names and laughing about things, Bobby said, "Let's call him Virgil. Like Virgil Runnels." And so Virgil it was. Dusty Rhodes's real name is Virgil Runnels. It was an inside wrestling rib on Dusty. It wasn't my idea, but when Virgil left World Wrestling Federation and joined me in WCW, they decided to call him Vincent, ribbing Vincent K. McMahon.

BOBBY "THE BRAIN" HEENAN:

At that time, Dusty Rhodes was the booker in Atlanta. He was burying everybody who was working in New York. So they needed a name for DiBiase's servant. I said, "How about Virgil?" Ted's finisher, the Million Dollar Dream, where he put his opponents to sleep, was named after Dusty. He called himself the American Dream. We got to kick Dusty in the balls twice. It was a good rib on Dusty (not that he wouldn't do it to us if he could). It was good fun.

Virgil and I became good friends. He was a heck of a nice guy and we spent a lot of time together. We initially thought that it would be a good idea to room together on the road. Unfortunately, it didn't work out because we needed our own space as well as control of the thermostat. One night, I woke up sweating bullets. I checked the thermostat and Virgil had turned it up to about eighty degrees. I turned the thing down all the way to zero degrees. I am a big guy and enjoy sleeping in cool temperatures. I got up in the morning and couldn't even see Virgil in his bed. He was buried under blanket on top of blanket. He said, "Man, I don't know if I can room with you. I can't handle sleeping in the cold."

"Ditto, brother, I love sleeping in the cold."

VIRGIL:

Ted is a great person. Even though we were on the road together every day, Ted and I never had an argument, nor did we get into one single fight. I didn't get along with my own family that well. He was like a brother to me. I even had the privilege to meet and get to know his family.

I signed a contract to be Ted's bodyguard. He treated me as a true professional. I did everything that was asked of me and never complained. I never viewed anything as demeaning and by no means ever took anything personal. I never cracked a smile, always staying in character. I did the job to the best of my ability.

One night we were staying at the Marriott Hotel Newark Airport. At that point, if it wasn't a major show or Pay-Per-View, Vince didn't want Virgil to drive me around in limousines but rather a Lincoln Town Car. After wrestling that evening, Virgil dropped me off at the front door. I said to him, "Don't worry about picking me up in the morning. I'm going to take the hotel shuttle to the airport and I will catch up with you at the gate." It was a break for him because he could then take the rental car directly to the airport and check it back in without worrying about dropping me off. When Virgil got to the gate the next day, I saw that his eye was swollen like someone had punched him. "Man, what happened to you?"

"Oh, man, I got up and had to use the bathroom in the middle of the night and accidentally ran into the door."

I didn't think anything about it until about a month or so later when I returned to the hotel. Virgil and I were on different flights. I ended up checking into the hotel by myself. As I was checking in, one of the bell guys came up to me (we were regulars there so I got to know most of the staff). He said, "So Ted, did Virgil ever get over that black eye after that air bag hit him in the head?"

"Air bag? What are you talking about?"

"Man, the last time you guys were here, Virgil went to take the car back. He got into the car and instead of backing up, he drove forward and ran right over the concrete block. The air bag shot out of the steering wheel and hit him right in the head. It gave him a black eye and a bloody lip."

That evening Virgil picked me up to take me to the arena. On the way there I asked him, "Hey, man, how is your lip and eye?"

"Oh, it's okay now."

"Hey, Virgil, that door you ran into didn't happen to look anything like an air bag, did it?"

His eyes got big and he said, "Who told you, man, who told you?" We just laughed.

VIRGIL:

I purchased a three-thousand-dollar Pelle black leather coat. Davey Boy Smith ribbed me real good by putting tape on the back of my jacket. When I went to remove the tape, the glue pulled the leather off. I was furious and immediately wanted to get back at Davey Boy. Ted convinced me to wait a while and get him a few weeks down the road. A few weeks later, Davey left his Union Jack flag cape unattended. I seized the moment and cut my name out of the back of the cape. It was perfect. Davey then tried to get me back by cutting my black pants. The pants he destroyed were actually Mr. Fuji's trousers.

I wrestled the Macho Man, Randy Savage, in a Steel Cage match in Madison Square Garden. There were no disqualifications, but the only way to win in that type of match was to escape from the cage by either climbing over the top or going through the door, and having both feet touch the ground. Throughout, we teased the fans with a tit-for-tat match. The final spot was for Randy to knock me out and climb over the top of the cage. As Randy headed up, Virgil came up from the outside to prevent him from leaving. Out of nowhere, a fan jumped the rail, climbed the cage, and tried to knock Virgil down. I screamed for Virgil to knock the fan down. He grabbed the guy by the head and threw him to the ground. Simultaneously, security and the police were there to arrest the guy. When we got back to the locker room, we had a good laugh.

In February of 1988, in front of a national televised audience, Andre the Giant defeated Hulk Hogan to win the title. The Million Dollar Man who could buy anything wanted the World Wrestling Federation Heavyweight title, so I purchased the title from Andre and became the new champion. World Wrestling Federation Commissioner Jack Tunney quickly stripped me of the title and ordered a tournament be held at *WrestleMania IV* to determine the new champion. It was my first *WrestleMania* and it was held at the Trump Plaza in Atlantic City. I even met Donald Trump and his then wife, Ivana.

In the tournament, I beat "Hacksaw" Jim Duggan and Don Muraco. After getting a bye in the semifinals because Hulk Hogan and Andre the Giant were disqualified in their match, I squared off against Randy Savage in the finals. With the help of Hulk Hogan, Randy pinned me around the ten-minute mark to become the new World Wrestling Federation Heavyweight Champion. The noise from the near-capacity crowd of over twenty thousand was deafening.

I was told that at *WrestleMania IV* I was going to win the title and become the champion. But Vince came up to me and told me that there was a change in plans. It seemed that there was an earlier dispute between the Honky Tonk Man and Randy Savage. In an effort to make everyone happy, Vince McMahon did what he had to do in the best interest of his company.

I would have loved to have been the champion. To have my name etched in stone with those who paved the way would have been a major accomplishment. But a heel champion is a transitional champion and he never holds the title for any major period of time. The fans wanted to come and cheer for their heroes. They wanted their champion to be the good guy, like Hulk Hogan. Winning the title isn't that important from a career standpoint.

When Vince told me that the plans had changed, he said, "Ted, you are the Million Dollar Man. What do you care about the title? It makes you an

The Macho Man and I always had great matches.

even bigger heel by losing. Afterward, you say you don't need the belt and we create your own title, the Million Dollar Belt. The way we will design it will put the heavyweight title to shame." I was now the biggest pompous ass in the industry and the fans hated me more than ever. I was so hated that my character was instrumental in turning many heels to babyfaces, such as Randy Savage, Hercules Hernandez, the Big Boss Man, and Jake "The Snake" Roberts.

TERRY FUNK:

The Million Dollar Man may have been Vince McMahon's idea, but I don't believe there was another person in the wrestling industry who could have been that character any better. He did a wonderful and marvelous job with it.

Teddy is a very unselfish individual. He also had respect for his opponent and the business. This is why Teddy did so well in the business, and I think Vince McMahon knew this about Teddy. And Teddy never held the heavyweight championship, which was a sign of him being a great worker. He could draw crowds and money without a championship title around his waist.

After *WrestleMania IV* and for the rest of 1988, I mainly wrestled in tag-team matches, partnered with Andre the Giant. It was a way for Andre to stay in the main events while protecting his injured back. Andre was a great friend. Most people didn't know he wrestled in pain. There were times when we walked to the ring together and he would have his hand on my shoulder to keep himself balanced. In the ring, I basically did all the work. Andre was very limited. Still, we had great tag-team matches against Hulk Hogan and a variety of guys. At the first-ever *SummerSlam* held at Madison Square Garden, we tagged for the match dubbed "Where the Mega-Powers Meet the Mega-Bucks." Former Minnesota governor and Superstar Jesse "the Body" Ventura was the guest referee. Randy's manager and then real-life wife, Elizabeth, moved away from her conservative nature and tore her skirt off to distract Ventura when victory was in our hands.

In March of 1988, Melanie gave birth to my third son, Brett. Although we are so blessed to have Brett today, at the time he was the proverbial accident. Another child was the furthest thing from our minds. In fact, Melanie was on birth control. But she caught a cold and was put on antibiotics. Unbeknownst to us, the antibiotics canceled out the pill. I will never forget the day we saw the sonogram. Melanie saw it first. She smiled and said, "I guess you got your way again." Sure enough, it was a boy!

I wanted to make sure that I was with Melanie before and after the baby was born. As it got closer to the due date, we decided that Melanie would have a cesarean section. I adjusted my schedule to make sure everything was in order. On March 16, with me by her side in the delivery room, Melanie gave birth to a healthy, seven-pound baby boy.

Later that year in Providence, I won the fourth King of the Ring tournament. I went through some great guys that night, first pinning Brutus Beefcake and then Ken Patera. In the semifinal, I was scheduled to face Ron Bass after he pinned none other than young and upcoming Superstar Shawn Michaels. But I paid off Ron Bass and he forfeited the match. I told the angry crowd, "Don't get upset with Ron Bass. He is no different than you. He did the same thing that anybody would do. He took the money. Just like him, everybody has a price for the Million Dollar Man."

Tim White, Andre's friend and handler, Virgil, and I would travel together. I enjoyed being with Andre. Besides eating and drinking a lot, we did everything first-class. He loved champagne and one night he ordered a hundred-dollar bottle of Dom Pérignon. Before the night was out, we had gone through ten bottles.

The more I traveled with Andre, the more I understood what he went through on a daily basis. He was a larger-than-life guy with a big heart, but he didn't have any private time. Where could a seven-four giant hide? People were constantly asking him for his autograph or to have their picture taken with him. It had come to the point where someone had to be with him at all times just to keep people away. One night, Andre and I were sitting at the lounge drinking a beer at the Marriott hotel in San Francisco. A woman came up to him. "Andre, Andre, will you please sign your autograph."

Andre replied, "No, not now."

She persisted and wouldn't take no for an answer. I finally stepped in and said, "Look, lady, everybody is entitled to their privacy. This is our time. Please come back in a little while."

In a snippy tone she replied, "Well, that isn't fair. I just attended the event and paid for a ticket to see you guys wrestle. I also spent money on T-shirts and even bought a video game. This is how you treat me?"

"I'm sorry you feel that way, but you got exactly what you paid for. You were entertained tonight. What you have to understand is that all the wrestlers are entitled to their privacy, including Andre. So it would be appreciated if you would simply leave."

It was amazing to me how indignant some people can get. They think that just because one is a celebrity, they have a right to intrude on that person's privacy. And they don't. Now, did Andre and I both sign autographs? Absolutely, yes! The fans are what the sport of wrestling is all about. But with respect to Andre, there came a time when he just quit signing. He was simply bombarded with too many requests.

The World Wrestling Federation work schedule was initially three weeks on and then a week off. I was in a different city every day and a different hotel every night. The schedule was then changed to ten days on, three days off, back on for four days, and then off for three again. In reality, we only got off six days a month.

HARLEY RACE:

Ted and I were both in World Wrestling Federation together. He was always congenial and we had respect for each other. He performed wonderfully in his role as the Million Dollar Man. His work in the ring was impeccable.

By early 1989, World Wrestling Federation was on an incredible roll. Vince McMahon's strategy was an overwhelming success. Some business schools throughout the country started using World Wrestling Federation as a case study. Vince had also started to market a vast array of wrestling games and toys, such as the action figures of me, Hulk Hogan, Randy Savage, Jake

Roberts, and the Brain Busters (Arn Anderson & Tully Blanchard). The Tonka toy company later introduced a soft, stuffed doll about eighteen inches tall called Wrestling Buddies. My youngest son, Brett, grew up with a doll of me by his side. World Wrestling Federation also launched its first-ever video arcade game as well as a video game for the Nintendo game system.

ARN ANDERSON:

One of the best ribs Teddy ever pulled on me was the "Ear in the Glass" rib. It was so famous that Bret Hart alluded to it in his 2006 WWE Hall of Fame speech. After a show in Salt Lake City, we had a little party at the bar in the Marriott hotel. I was leaving World Wrestling Federation, so it was sort of a going-away party. We were drinking and having a good time. Teddy was there with Tully Blanchard, Bret Hart, Terry Taylor, and a bunch of the guys. One of Teddy's fraternity buddies from college, Mad Dog, was also there. He was the equipment manager for the West Texas football team. He also had a prosthetic ear. I guess when I left to use the bathroom, Teddy took the guy's ear off and put it in the bottom of my sea-breeze drink. Without me looking, Teddy led a toast wishing me success, calling a salute, and everybody drank. As I drank, something hit the top of my teeth. I looked in the glass and there was a man's ear. I couldn't believe it. I started spewing and puking from the bar all the way to the front door. They all had a good laugh, and I have to admit, it was infamous in the annals of ribs for achieving its desired effect!

I started off 1989 wrestling in the thirty-man *Royal Rumble* held in Houston. At the live Pay-Per-View, I drew number twenty-two. I didn't like the number. Using my status and wealth, I consulted the manager of the Big Boss Man and Akeem, the Slickster. I made him an offer that he couldn't refuse and swapped picks to attain position number thirty. Unfortunately, I was eliminated by Big John Studd. For the next four years, I had a horrible streak of losses at the *Royal Rumble*.

The *Royal Rumble 1990* was held in Orlando. I knew I was going to be part of the event and didn't think that I would wrestle more than five or ten minutes. So I went out with the boys, partying at Church Street Station and other area bars. I definitely had drunk more than I should have. I arrived at the arena and felt very light-headed. I thought to myself, "Thank goodness I'm wrestling in the *Rumble*. There is no way I could wrestle for more than fifteen minutes." Pat Patterson came up to me and said, "Ted, don't eat too much today. You are going to be in the *Rumble* a long time." I smiled and thought he was teasing me. Pat quickly added, "No, no, Ted. I am serious. You are going to be in there for nearly an hour."

PAT PATTERSON:

I created the *Royal Rumble.* Years ago, somewhere in the business somebody came up with the idea of the regular battle royal. I always wanted to come up with an idea for the business. The *Royal Rumble* involved thirty guys, beginning with two men in the ring, and every ninety seconds or two minutes someone else would enter. The guys loved working the event.

At first, Vince didn't fully believe in it. He thought an hour would be too long. The first *Royal Rumble* was held in Hamilton, Ontario, as a special on the USA Network. The results were huge ratings. Television-wise, it was a very successful night. It is now an annual Pay-Per-View event held every January.

Since I purchased the final spot at the previous year's *Royal Rumble*, the creative team decided to have some fun with the Million Dollar Man. With a national audience watching, I was stunned when I drew the first spot in the *Rumble*. The interviewer said, "It looks like the Million Dollar Man's money didn't work for him this year. He is number one!" I went out and wrestled for a record forty-four minutes and forty-seven seconds until I was eliminated by the Ultimate Warrior. After the match, I was completely exhausted.

At first, I had no problem with the Ultimate Warrior. He had a great body, but his wrestling skills were limited. Vince McMahon wanted to market his look. As a person who grew up in the industry and respected it, I just believed that the Ultimate Warrior didn't appreciate the opportunity. He was even made the champion. I didn't believe that he gave his all to the company.

The Ultimate Warrior wasn't a good technical wrestler and he lacked charisma. There have been many guys in the business who weren't good workers, such as JYD, but he had charisma and, more important, he respected the profession. Vince helped the Warrior get over by putting him in the ring with guys who could make him look good: me, Jake Roberts, and Hulk Hogan. All of his matches with Hogan were a credit to Hogan's wrestling. But the Ultimate Warrior never became a student of the business and never appreciated anybody who tried to help him, including me.

Very rarely did I leave the ring angry. When I wrestled the Warrior one time in Japan, I left the ring mad. Right after he became champion, World Wrestling Federation went on a tour of Japan. Vince put me in a match with the Warrior in the sold-out Egg Dome to make him look good. I had no problem doing that, but I did get upset by the way it turned out.

Having wrestled in Japan, I was familiar with the style. I let the Warrior know that our match should be more serious and less animated than in the States. For the first ten minutes of the match, I made him look like a wrestling god. I bumped all over the ring and absorbed all of his power spots. When my turn came to make a comeback, the referee told me that time had been cut and the match had to end. In front of a capacity crowd, I got squashed by the Warrior. I never asked or found out why, but I was clearly mad.

One example of his self-centeredness was when I was invited to do an autograph session in New York a few years ago. There were other wrestlers that attended, including the Ultimate Warrior. All the wrestlers were together in a room and we signed autographs and sold our gimmicks. A few fans asked about the Warrior and wondered where he was. I didn't pay attention but noticed he wasn't in the room. I was told, "The Warrior said he didn't want to be in the same room with the other wrestlers signing autographs. He wanted his own room, space, and table." His pompous attitude was typical.

If the Warrior had been more personable, and appreciated what the boys tried to do to help him, I would have had no problem with him. But he didn't. If it wasn't for everyone else who worked their tails for him, he would have never made it in World Wrestling Federation.

The *Royal Rumble 1992* in Albany, New York, was one of my easiest paydays ever, but the end result made all the fans in attendance and watching on Pay-Per-View very happy. Based on my history in the *Rumble*, the creative team decided to do something different with my character. The British Bulldog drew the first spot and I got the second. Before the commentators could even share our stats with the viewers, I was eliminated in slightly more than one minute. The loss would soon spearhead me into tag team wrestling.

Since I couldn't win or buy the World Wrestling Federation title, the storyline then had me purchasing my own championship title. I unveiled the Million Dollar Belt in 1989. It was designed and made by Terry Betteridge of Betteridge Jewelers in Greenwich, Connecticut. He is a world-renowned gemologist. The fans were told that it was made of real gold and laced with

hundreds of real diamonds in the shape of three large dollar signs. It wasn't. The belt was gold-plated and all of the stones were cubic zirconia. But on the back of the belt, there were three tiny authentic diamonds. I asked Vince, "Why are those three diamonds back there?"

"They are real diamonds."

"Why are they back there? Nobody is ever going to see them."

"Well, Ted, we just want to keep you honest. When anybody asks you if the diamonds in the belt are real and you say yes, well, you aren't lying."

According to the documents that I carried for the belt whenever I went through customs, its estimated value was about forty thousand dollars. In all of my years that I carried the belt, I was never asked to show papers. Though I have a replica of the belt, the actual one is locked in a safe. It should be noted that the belt was never an official title and thus wasn't ever sanctioned by World Wrestling Federation.

TERRY TAYLOR:

In an effort to be part of World Wrestling Federation, I used to call Pat Patterson every Friday at noon for nine months straight. I had a new son and I needed to work. I also really wanted to be in World Wrestling Federation. When Teddy got hired as the Million Dollar Man, I called him and asked if he could help me out. I told Teddy I had been trying to get in for some nine months. Sometimes Pat would answer, but most of the time I got an answering machine. Teddy understood and said he would go to bat for me and talk to Pat. And he did.

Soon thereafter, I called Pat one Friday at noon for like the fortieth time. This time Pat answered and said, "Yeah, yeah, yeah, I know you are just looking for an opportunity."

"You don't even know who this is."

"Yes, I do. You have been calling here every Friday at noon for almost a year. If you promise to never call again, I'll give you a chance to come to TV on Monday." Thanks, Teddy!

I also want to say that I am lucky Teddy was around because

he has the largest head in the business. I can't believe the size of that melon. If it wasn't for him, I probably would have that honor. Thanks again, Teddy!

There is an old saying in wrestling, "There are big stars and there are good hands. And the good hands never make any money, because they are making the big stars into big stars." I think Teddy is one of the first guys to ever be a good hand that became a big star. Because he could get a great match out of anybody—he was big, athletic, and could talk as good as anybody on the microphone. Teddy meant a whole lot to the business and gave a whole lot back. Not many people can say that.

In mid-1989, I started an angle with Jake Roberts. It initially started when Jake and Andre got into a program. Andre had interfered in one of Jake's matches. As Andre was beating Jake down, Jake sought help from his snake, Damien. Jake let his snake out of the bag and Andre hightailed it out of the ring. It was obvious that Andre was scared of snakes. I voiced my opinion about Jake and the next thing I knew, Jake started using Damien to scare Virgil and me. After a match at a television taping of *Superstars of Wrestling* Jake pinned Virgil. When his back was turned, I jumped him from behind and administered a series of piledrivers. I had broken his neck, putting him out of commission for a few months. He actually had already needed surgery on his neck, so the angle gave him an opportunity to take some time off.

We re-ignited our program in March of 1990. Jake returned to wreak havoc on me and Virgil. He even stole my Million Dollar Belt. We finally ended the program at *WrestleMania VI.* The event was held in Toronto, Canada. A new attendance record was set when 67,678 people packed in the SkyDome. After roughly twelve minutes, I defeated Jake by a countout to regain the Million Dollar Belt.

My contest at *WrestleMania VI* was probably one of my most enjoyable matches, simply because it was a really good match and it was very easy to work with Jake. We didn't have to talk that much in the ring or plan things in advance. It just came together. Jake had great ring psychology. In my estimation, if Jake would have kept himself clean, I believe that he would right now be in Stamford working for Vince McMahon on the creative team.

In the summer of 1990, I started a program with the "American Dream" Dusty Rhodes. Back then, he was dressed in yellow polka dots and called the Common Man. Vince completely changed him from the character that made him a Superstar in the NWA. They put him in this awkward outfit and assigned him a heavyset African-American manager, Sapphire. I think the change was a test by Vince to see if Dusty could be a team player. Dusty was great to work with in the ring and we had some very good matches together.

Anyway, we feuded for about six months, which started with me buying Sapphire's services at *SummerSlam* and ended when Virgil and I beat Dusty and his son Dustin. I pinned Dusty with a roll-up. After the match, I demanded that Virgil wrap the Million Dollar Belt around my waist. Virgil picked it up, but instead of putting it around my waist, he hit me with the belt right upside my head. Immediately, I started an angle with Virgil and he instantly became a babyface.

TERRY FUNK:

The Dusty Rhodes–Ted DiBiase feud didn't work out because Vince gave Dusty a horseshit, polka-dot gimmick that nobody could get over with.

Virgil wasn't the best worker in the business. When we started our program, I had to be at my best. For us to have a match at *WrestleMania VII* in 1991 and work at the highest level was truly a testament to Virgil's desire to listen and let me lead. He was very coachable and ended up wrestling a lot of good matches. The match's success had a lot to do with the presence of Roddy Piper. In the end, even though my new valet, Sensational Sherri, was in my corner, I lost to Virgil. I was counted out after attacking Roddy Piper outside the ring. The story line crowned Virgil as the new Million Dollar Champion.

VIRGIL:

I learned the psychology aspect of the wrestling business from Ted. In fact, there is no better teacher than Ted when it comes to the psychology of the business, overall wrestling ability, and speaking skills. He is the best.

Working with Ted was unbelievable. There is no better field general than Teddy. He was one of the best wrestlers ever in the business. He is in a class by himself.

Sherri Martel was a wonderful person and we worked perfectly together. She had a storied wrestling career and worked for every major federation in the United States. She was a great wrestler and became the Women's Champion in both World Wrestling Federation and the now defunct American Wrestling Association (AWA). She was just as awesome a manager, having managed numerous top-named guys such as Ric Flair, Shawn Michaels, and Randy Savage. Because of her impact and success in the sport, in 2006, I inducted Sherri into the WWE Hall of Fame. It was unfortunate that she passed away in June of 2007 at forty-nine.

Given that Piper had interfered in my matches against Virgil, we started a program. Roddy Piper is a great guy and an excellent worker. We had many good matches together. Before the start of each match, I would get on the microphone and say, "You know, I really don't feel like wrestling tonight. It's been a long trip and I don't feel like breaking a sweat. Roddy Piper, I know you don't want to be embarrassed by me in front of all these people. Because Roddy, if we wrestle tonight, you will be embarrassed. So to save you from being humiliated by the Million Dollar Man in front of this crowd, I am going to offer you three hundred dollars. Take the money and go out and have a fine meal and order a nice bottle of wine. What do you say?" When I'd turn away, Piper would punch me and the money would go flying up in the air. He nailed me a few more times until I landed outside the ring on the concrete floor. While I was dazed, Piper scooped up the money and handed it to the fans in the front row. I went crazy and screamed, "That is my money! Don't give the fans my money!"

At an event in Sacramento, I decided to have some fun with the angle.

Roddy Piper just didn't appreciate my offers to spare him.

Melanie traveled with me to the show because we had just visited my step-sister, who lived roughly eighty miles from the venue in Napa Valley. My stepsister wanted to come to the show. So I got them two ringside tickets. In all the years that I have been in the business, my wife has never sat in the front row; she was either in the dressing room area or in the cheap seats.

With my gimmick, everything operated on the honor system. I never wasted or abused the company's money. But this one time, I thought that my wife and stepsister should have the three hundred dollars. We were going to use the money to have a nice meal after the show. Nobody would know the difference.

Prior to the match, I spoke to Piper in the dressing room. "Look, Roddy, when we do this thing tonight and you roll out of the ring to give away the money, I want you to give it to my wife. She will be sitting in the front row.

Nobody knows that she is my wife. So when you get the money, roll out of the ring and slap the money in her hands. Tonight, we will all go out and have a good time." Piper agreed.

Piper followed everything perfectly and put the money in my wife's hands. After the conclusion of our match, we joked about it in the locker room and planned to go out for a nice little meal together. After showering, we met up with my wife and stepsister. I asked Melanie if she had the money. She looked at me with an angry pout. "No. Don't you ever do that to me again. When Roddy put the money in my hand, and then walked away, people started coming from everywhere. They started grabbing and reaching for the money. It was unbearable. I thought they were going to trample me, so I just let it go. Don't get any other harebrained ideas like that again or I'm going to kill you!"

It would be some five years before I would run into Piper again backstage at a house show in Kansas City. After the show, we went back to our hotel. We were both staying at the Marriott by the airport. Before settling in, we decided to go to a local pub down the road to have a few beers for old times' sake. I remember saying, "What trouble can we get into?" Sure enough, after about ten minutes, some guy said something obnoxious to me. I tried blowing it off so as not to start any trouble. But the guy was being quite repulsive. Piper is a pretty scrappy guy. He is well known for losing his cool and is very successful at bar fights. Right before I was about to grab the guy by the throat, Piper came from out of nowhere and started beating the guy up. He actually laid him out.

I regained my title by defeating Virgil with the help of the Repo Man. When I became a Tag Team Champion a few months later, the angle allowed me to put the Million Dollar Belt in hibernation. It wasn't until four years later when I was managing Steve Austin that the title came back into play. Since he was my protégé, I simply gave him the belt and started calling him the champ.

PAT PATTERSON:

I don't even have a clue where the belt is today. A few years ago, I recall someone asking where the Million Dollar Belt was. Nobody could find it. I am sure Vince has it somewhere locked away.

At the *King of the Ring 1991,* I wrestled Ricky Steamboat to a draw. Ricky was one of those wrestlers whose work in the ring I sincerely admired. As chance happened, that night in Providence was the only time I ever wrestled Ricky. We had an excellent match and I remember telling him how enjoyable it was to work with him. The event also marked when Mike Rotundo (I.R.S.—Irwin R. Schyster) started getting a push as one of the major heels in the company. Toward the end of 1991, creative decided that I needed to enter into tag-team wrestling.

MIKE ROTUNDO (I.R.S.):

Since Ted basically worked in the Mid-South territory and me in Florida and the Carolinas, we never crossed paths until we were in World Wrestling Federation. We hit it off instantly. The creative team soon decided to team us together as Money Inc. They thought we would fit well together with Ted's Million Dollar Man gimmick and my deal as the I.R.S. It was a great move because we worked very well together and had a tremendous amount of success.

We wrestled many great tag teams such as the Natural Disasters, the Steiner Brothers, the Beverly Brothers, the Nasty Boys, the Mega Maniacs (Brutus Beefcake & Hulk Hogan), and the Legion of Doom. In February of 1992 we defeated the Legion of Doom (aka the Road Warriors) to become the Tag Team Champions. We went on to be three-time World Wrestling Federation Tag Team Champions.

The Road Warriors were one of the most popular tag teams in the world. I was friends with both Animal and the late Hawk. I will never forget our match that year at the *SummerSlam 1992* event. In front of eighty-thousand-plus fans in Wembley Stadium in London, we lost to the Legion of Doom after Animal pinned me to secure the victory. It is a fact that World Wrestling Federation sold out Wembley Stadium faster than anybody, including the Beatles.

STEVE KEIRN:

Teddy, in his peers' eyes, is one of the greatest wrestlers that ever came through the business. I personally put Teddy and those other second-generation wrestlers at the highest level. They were introduced to the business at an early age, knew the terminology, and respected the profession. As the Million Dollar Man, he made a name for himself. The promotion makes you the star, but you have to be able to carry the ball once they hand it to you. When Vince gave him the Million Dollar Man opportunity, Teddy didn't only run with the ball, he stole it. He shined brighter than many stars have ever shined. In the ring, he gave a hundred percent and never went to the ring with an attitude that he was just going to get by. He was a complete professional and will forever be a legend in the sport of professional wrestling.

It was a very exciting time in wrestling in 1993. *Raw* started airing on the USA Network. *Raw* was an unprecedented TV show shot in front of a live au-

On *Raw* with Vince and I.R.S.

dience. We also started doing tours overseas. I wrestled in England, Ireland, Scotland, and Germany. No matter what country we were in, every venue was packed with screaming fans.

During that time, good ol' J.R. joined Vince McMahon and Jerry Lawler doing the announcing duties on *Raw* and Pay-Per-View events. It was probably one of Vince's best hires ever. Jim is the greatest announcer in the history of professional wrestling. I have known him for years and remember him calling a World Heavyweight Championship match between me and Ric Flair in the mid-1980s when I was in the Mid-South/UWF territory.

JIM ROSS:

The Million Dollar Man persona is one for the ages, and you can take that to the bank . . . no pun intended. A creation of Vince McMahon and Ted DiBiase, the Million Dollar Man was someone anyone could identify with on varying levels—no matter their background—on any continent. Ted was perfect for the role because he could naturally outwrestle most opponents, who were usually fan favorites, and then robustly laugh in the face of the popular Superstar and the Superstar's fans. I would suggest that the Million Dollar Man was one of the top ten all-time great characters WWE ever featured, and in the top five of antagonists. The Million Dollar Man's exploits will live for generations to come, and if I ever had to draft wrestlers to start my own company, the Million Dollar Man would be a surefire first rounder. Wrestlers have to fit roles and roles have to fit wrestlers. Ted DiBiase was the perfect choice for the Million Dollar Man, who the fans just knew was laughing all the way to the bank.

NIKITA KOLOFF:

Ted's wrestling skills and abilities speak for themselves in terms of his success in the wrestling industry. He was great on the microphone and had great psychology for the business—an art that I believe had long been lost. He portrayed the Million Dollar Man gimmick extremely well and had great success with the character.

It was about this time that my drinking and partying was getting out of control. From the late-night drinking to the infidelity, I started to believe that I was the Million Dollar Man. My ego was out of control, more so my drinking. Because of my celebrity status, I was invited to party after party. One time in Germany, Ric Flair and I were at a local bar near the venue. Our fans were packed into the bar and we both were enjoying the attention. Ric left to go to the bathroom, and a young lady came up to me and engaged in small talk. She was very cordial; I would find out she was an undercover police officer. All of a sudden, everyone in the bar heard "Wooooo!" Ric was headed toward me, in nothing but his socks and underwear. Before I could wise him up, he said, "Hi, honey. How would you like to ride Space Mountain?" The look on Ric's face when I told him that she was a police officer is permanently etched in my mind.

A few years earlier, I was fortunate to have the opportunity to have introduced to the wrestling world maybe the most extraordinary wrestler in the history of WWE, Undertaker. He was part of my Million Dollar Team on Thanksgiving Day at the *Survivor Series 1990* at the Hartford Civic Center. It was a four-on-four elimination match where we challenged Dusty's Dream Team. His team consisted of him, Koko B. Ware, and the Hart Foundation.

For weeks I teased the fans that I would have a mystery partner with my two other teammates—the Honky Tonk Man and Greg Valentine. After we made our way to the ring, the crowd eagerly awaited him. The fans were in awe when Undertaker made his way down to the ring. Even to this day, his entrance into the ring is one of the most entertaining moments in the business. He eliminated Dusty Rhodes but subsequently got himself eliminated when he followed Dusty to the back. My team won the match after I pinned Bret Hart.

Bret and I go way back to my college days at West Texas State. I met him and a few of his brothers when they came to Amarillo to visit the Funks. I admired his wrestling talent and pleasant personality. The two of us got along well because of what we had in common: mutual love and respect for the business. We were second-generation wrestlers and both of our fathers were shooters. Bret's dad, Stu, had a tough reputation and would train people in the basement of his house, which he called the dungeon.

After we visited in Amarillo, I didn't see Bret again until I started working for Vince. Unfortunately, we didn't wrestle each other that often because we were both heels. We wrestled once in Los Angeles and it was probably one of the best matches I ever had in World Wrestling Federation. Bret had great technical skills and ring psychology. Bret was one of the greatest wrestlers in the history of World Wrestling Federation.

About a month before *WrestleMania IX*, my grandma was rushed to the hospital. I hopped on a plane to Tucson and prayed that she would still be alive when I arrived. She was. As I prayed for and held the hands of the woman who had raised me, hundreds of images scrolled through my mind—from the fun times I had hanging out at her restaurant to the constant love she gave me.

Grandma was my anchor.

I couldn't believe she was dying. Despite the fact that Grandma continued to fight for a couple more months at home, she eventually slipped into a coma. As she lay there, I kept saying, "Grandma, I love you." I'll never forget the look in her beautiful eyes. She eventually passed away at the age of eighty-nine.

Although 1992 and 1993 were exciting years for me in wrestling, the grind of the schedule and lifestyle affected me personally. Being a champion and at the top of my game gave me fame and fortune. But it would end up being one of the worst times in my life. At the pinnacle of my success, I was personally out of control. I let all the notoriety and money go to my head. My life was wrestling, drinking, and women. In fact, after *WrestleMania VIII*, I partied all night long. I didn't even sleep. That next morning, I took a limousine to the Detroit airport to begin our European tour. I called Melanie to check in. It was then that she confronted me about my infidelity.

I had to face up and take a long, hard look at myself. Because of my indiscretions, I put in jeopardy everything that I worked my tail off for. I disrespected myself, my wife, and my family. It was time to take responsibility and drastically change my life.

HAL SANTOS (friend and pastor):

I have known Teddy for some thirty years and he is one of my best friends. But in March of 1992, I had to be more than his friend. As a pastor, Teddy called me and told me that he really messed up with Melanie. After Teddy confided in me, I hung up with him, telling him to call me back in about an hour. He was in Europe at the time. I then called Melanie. I guess she thought it was Ted calling, because she hung up on me. I finally got her to listen to me and we chatted. She was very hurt. Teddy called me back and I said, "Okay, Teddy. I spoke to Melanie. She is very hurt but agreed to meet with us at my house in Fairview Heights, Illinois, tomorrow. You need to come home so we can work on getting your marriage back together." Ted was at my house the next evening.

As we sat in the living room of my home I said to Ted,

"Whatever you do, before you say anything, the Bible states that the truth will set you free. It doesn't say it is painless. But it does guarantee that if you speak the truth, God will help you." They started talking it through and started working it out. Their boys came to the house a few days later and they stayed about three weeks at my place. We even took a trip to Chicago with my youth group. It was at that time that Teddy made a commitment, with his wife and family, to Jesus Christ. After lots of counseling, prayer, trust, and time, Teddy and Melanie worked out all their problems.

About three months before *WrestleMania IX*, I walked into Vince McMahon's office and gave him my notice that I had planned to leave World Wrestling Federation. I really respected Vince and he had done so much for me and my career. But my faith wasn't strong enough to keep me from being dragged back into my old ways. My marriage was at stake. After a lengthy conversation, Vince accepted my decision to leave and wished me the best of luck.

My last match as a wrestler for World Wrestling Federation was at

Razor trying to break my hold.

SummerSlam in August of 1993. Since I was leaving to get my personal life back in order, I once again helped turn another heel into a babyface. So for the next few weeks I.R.S. and I had tag-team and single matches against Razor Ramon and the 1-2-3 Kid. The program and my wrestling career with World Wrestling Federation ended in front of twenty-four thousand people at the Palace in Auburn Hills. It was there that Razor Ramon pinned me around the eight-minute mark.

MIKE ROTUNDO (I.R.S.):

Ted and I were working a program against the Natural Disasters (Typhoon & Earthquake). For some reason, Typhoon didn't show up for the match. So I worked a singles match against Earthquake (John Tenta). The finish was supposed to have Ted come down and throw in my metal suitcase so I could use it to knock out Earthquake. I don't know why, but Ted ended up coming in late. While Earthquake got ready to cover me for the pin, Ted was making his way down to the ring. Since Ted wasn't close enough to stop the count, he just slung the metal briefcase into the ring, hitting the referee, Earl Hebner, in the head. The referee wasn't completely knocked out cold, but after he disqualified me, he left the ring slightly loopy. After the match, the doctors had to tend to Earl.

Ted and I always had a lot of fun and laughs on the road. One time, however, our enjoyment cost Ted some of his own money. After a show in upstate New York, Ted and I missed our exit off the freeway as we headed to our hotel. It was dark and there wasn't anybody on the road. After a few miles, we saw a sign that showed the next exit was some thirty miles away. We didn't see anyone on the road. Ted decided to make a U-turn. About a half mile down the road, we heard and saw the blue lights. A New York state trooper pulled us over and issued Ted a ticket.

13

COMMENTATOR AND MANAGER

Avoiding the lifestyle I had embraced by wrestling in Japan seemed like a good idea. I hadn't counted on injuring my neck. I had to be at home for at least three months, with nothing to do. I was concerned about my future, but I was very happy to be at home with my wife and kids. I was able to enjoy the Thanksgiving, Christmas, and New Year's holidays with my family.

All of my financial obligations were being met. Due to good investments and savings, I had a steady income. But it was nominal and I knew it was only a matter of time before I had to start working again. I was having fun. I was busy spending all my time with my three boys, Michael, seventeen, Teddy, twelve, and Brett, seven. They were growing up way too fast and I had lots of lost time to make up for.

That Thanksgiving, our family spent a wonderful week with my in-laws on their ninety-acre wooded home right outside of Crystal Springs, Mississippi. My in-laws are fantastic people and my father-in-law was like a dad to my kids when I was on the road. The boys call him Pop. That weekend Pop, the boys, and I had a great time fishing and hunting. It was quite amazing to watch them teach me how to properly bait a hook and aim a rifle.

I was sitting in a deer stand one early morning, and I was taken aback by the quietness of the woods. As I stared into the open sky, I became overwhelmed by the moment. The tranquillity brought forth a sense of inner peace. It made me realize that I needed to relax more often and stop to smell the roses. Ever since 1975, I had been going nonstop. The moment of reflection struck a chord and I realized I had missed out on way too much with my family.

But after the holidays, I started getting antsy. I was enjoying the time off, but I just couldn't do nothing. Because of my neck injury, I knew that my

My three sons (from left to right): Teddy, Michael, and Brett.

days in the ring were over. But I figured that I could do something else. I sat down with Melanie and kicked around a variety of ideas. The one thing that we agreed on was for me to pursue a career doing voice-over work. Like my biological father, Ted, I have a very deep, bass voice. People have told me for years that I would be good at providing voice-overs in radio and TV commercials. So I decided to go to Hollywood and pursue a career.

While making all the arrangements, I decided to call my good friend who lives in Los Angeles, Rich Minzer. He worked in the corporate offices of Gold's Gym. If anyone wanted to open a Gold's Gym franchise, Rich was the contact person. He had lots of friends in the wrestling business and would come to many of the matches.

I told Rich I was going out to L.A. to try my hand at voice-over work and was going to take some lessons. I also wanted to see if he would train me and help me get back into shape. While I was relaxing over the holidays, I had put on about twenty pounds. I didn't go to the gym or watch what I was eating.

I also called my biological father, Ted. I told him that I was coming into town, and he insisted that I stay with him. For years, I had unsuccessfully tried to get him to move to Mississippi. He had a nice one-bedroom apartment located about six blocks from where he worked at the ABC studios. He loved living in Los Angeles and he enjoyed the Hollywood lifestyle.

I arrived in Los Angeles in January of 1994 and enrolled in voice-over classes. Although I wanted Melanie and the boys to be with me, they couldn't be there because of school. I was going to miss her and the kids deeply, but I had to do something to make a living and provide for them.

I started working out with Rich. He introduced me to another trainer, Francois, who performed Shiatsu on me, a form of Japanese therapy of physical and energy rebalance. It raised my energy level and increased my flexibility. I also did extensive strength training and cardiovascular work. After one month of training and watching my caloric intake, I lost all the weight that I had gained over the holidays. In fact, I was in the best shape of my life.

I found out that a Hollywood career would be challenging and very competitive. To get a chance in the voice-over profession, I was going to have to invest a lot of energy, resources, and time. It would be like starting an entirely new career. I was going to turn forty, and I wasn't about to commit the next five years of my life to pursuing something that might never materialize at the expense of my family and faith. I decided voice-over work wasn't in my future.

I spent a lot of quality time with Ted. At the time, he had emphysema and was on oxygen twenty-four hours a day. His mobility was limited and my stay gave me an opportunity to help him out around the house, running errands and driving him around town. He took me out to celebrate my fortieth birthday. I was even there when the 1994 Northridge earthquake hit.

On January 17, I was awakened by the shaking of the apartment building. After getting my bearings, I rolled over and grabbed both sides of the bed. While holding on, the bed's headboard fell off. It hit me right on the head. By the time I realized what had happened, it was over. Although I had felt a couple of tremors while I was wrestling in Japan, this was my first major earthquake experience. The damage was widespread. Sections of the freeways had collapsed, as did parking structures and office buildings.

After the earthquake, I immediately checked on Ted to make sure he was all right. We were both fine. Although the apartment building didn't suffer any structural damage, the inside was a complete mess. Dishes and cups were broken and the contents of the refrigerator were on the floor. The TV broke, as did most of his appliances. It was a good thing that I was there, because in his condition there would have been no way he could have cleaned up that mess. It was an unforgettable experience.

MELANIE:

I like to tease Ted that while he was in Hollywood pursuing a voice-over career, when he turned forty the earth shook.

One afternoon when I was spending time with Ted at the apartment, I received a call from Bruce Prichard. After we exchanged some small talk he said, "Vince wants to know if you would be interested in coming back to World Wrestling Federation to cohost the *Royal Rumble*."

"You are talking about commentating, right?"

"Yes."

"Who would I be cohosting the *Rumble* with?"

"Vince."

I wasn't too sure what to think or what to do. "Vince does know that I have never commentated before, right?"

Bruce replied, "Yes, Ted, Vince knows. Come out here and give it a try. Just be the Million Dollar Man and do your own thing. Vince will lead you through the show and help you out."

"Okay, I'll give it a try." I called Melanie and she thought it was a great opportunity and supported my decision.

When I got back home, I called Bruce and we discussed the particulars and terms. The next day, I flew to Boston, rented a car, and drove to Providence, where the *Royal Rumble* was being held. Once I arrived at the Providence Civic Center, I met with Bruce and some of the boys. I had been away from the company for almost six months and there was a lot of new talent. Bruce then took me to meet with Vince and the production team. For about three hours, I was instructed about the technical aspects and I learned a lot about how to effectively commentate. I was a tad nervous, but Vince kept me relaxed.

Vince and I worked well together. Throughout the show, Vince kept reassuring me, reminding me to just be myself. Together we called three championship matches, which included a Casket match between champion Yokozuna and Undertaker—with the help of ten guys, Yokozuna retained the title. The ending of the King of the Ring tournament was quite spectacular. They crowned two kings, Bret Hart and Lex Luger, because they both landed on the floor simultaneously.

Afterward, Vince and I discussed the evening's event. I asked him about my performance. "For a first time, you did okay." I appreciated the positive support and thanked him for the opportunity. Then I added, "Vince, ever since I suffered my neck injury and can't wrestle, I'd had no idea what I was going to do. If you really like my commentating, I would be more than happy to do more. I will also be happy to come back to the company in the role of a manager or anything else you would like for me to do."

Vince smiled and said, "Let me think about it and I will get back to you in a few days."

That night at the hotel, I pondered my future with World Wrestling Federation. I had a good feeling about Vince bringing me back on board, but I wasn't a hundred percent sure.

A couple of days later, while Melanie and I were eating breakfast, the phone rang. It was Bruce Prichard. "Hey, Ted. Vince wants you to go to *WrestleMania X* and make a cameo appearance. I'm not sure about anything else, but you can visit with Vince when you get there." I accepted the offer.

WrestleMania X took place in New York City at Madison Square Garden. It was an awesome card and I really enjoyed the Ladder match for the Intercontinental title between Shawn Michaels and Razor Ramon. It was the first time World Wrestling Federation had televised a Ladder match and both men did a fantastic job. Another match that stood out was between Bret and Owen Hart. They grappled for some twenty minutes, which is something that many workers can't do today.

As for me, the creative team decided to have me sit in the crowd. Next to me was a President Bill Clinton look-alike. Throughout the show, the

camera would show me and "President Clinton" laughing and hamming it up. The announcers would make many references to me and the president being good friends; they wondered if I had bought him off and whether I had stayed in the White House. I had fun with the impersonator. He did a great job with the antics and mannerisms. He had the real President Clinton down to a T.

After the show, I went to the hotel lounge and had beer with the boys. When I turned in, about two in the morning, the telephone rang. It was Bruce Prichard. "Hey, Ted. Vince wants to know if you want to permanently try television commentating."

"Absolutely!"

"Great. Get some rest because tomorrow a limo is going to pick you up at seven and take you to the studio in Stamford."

"You mean as in five hours from now?"

Bruce chuckled. "Yeah, so get some sleep and I'll see you in the morning." I quickly called Melanie and shared with her the great news. I was so excited that I didn't get much sleep that night.

The limo took me to the studio and I met with Vince. We agreed on the terms of a contract and I started my professional wrestling television commentating career. In 1994, for the first time, I had become a salaried employee. I wasn't making as much as I had been wrestling, but it was a decent wage.

It was also a good deal because I didn't have to spend a lot of time on the road. I only had to be at TV tapings two days every three weeks. Every week, I would go to the studio in Stamford and work all day doing voice-overs for World Wrestling Federation television shows.

For the next two years, I did the color commentating on a variety of shows. I did a few shows with Stan Lane but was quickly partnered with Gorilla Monsoon. Gorilla was a legend in professional wrestling as a worker, booker, and announcer. He was a standout high school and college athlete. Standing six-five and weighing close to four hundred pounds, Gorilla held a few Tag Team Championships and was inducted into the WWE Hall of Fame in 1994. Five years later he passed away at sixty-two.

I truly admired Gorilla. He was a quality human being who had a big heart. He went out of his way to help me in the announcer's booth. I thought we were a great team, and it was all because of Gorilla. A good color commentator is only as good as the play-by-play announcer, and Gorilla was the best.

Color commentating gave me the opportunity to look at the wrestling business from a different perspective. I had been a referee and wrestler, and because of those two positions I had a better understanding of the sport. But now I understood the entire process. Doing color really made me appreciate the hours upon hours of work that the production team put into filming, editing, and scripting the shows.

Even though I was in the announcer's booth, Vince also wanted me to become a manager. Vince said, "Ted, you are still quite over with the fans. They hate you and I think your role as a manager will help some of the new heels get over with the fans." I agreed and accepted the additional responsibility. I immediately formed the Million Dollar Corporation, which lasted from April 1994 to May 1996. During that time, I managed guys like I.R.S., Nikolai Volkoff, Tatanka, King Kong Bundy, Sid Vicious, and Bam Bam Bigelow.

Bam Bam Bigelow was a great guy. He had an intimidating look, with fire tattoos all over his head and body, but he was a gentle giant. He was one of the most agile workers that I had ever seen for a man his size. Bigelow weighed close to four hundred pounds and could do a cartwheel like a gymnast. His moonsault off the top rope was mind-boggling. Bigelow worked for every major promotion in the States and even was a Tag Team Champion in New Japan. It was unfortunate that he died from an apparent drug overdose in 2007 at forty-five.

A huge angle was set up between Bigelow and New York Giants football player Lawrence "LT" Taylor. LT is regarded as one of the greatest linebackers in the history of the NFL. It was a huge deal with the press because of the popularity of LT, especially in the New York area. Bigelow and LT worked a short program setting up their match at *WrestleMania XI*. During a match at the *Royal Rumble 1995* Bigelow, who lost the match, was mocked at ringside by LT. Bigelow didn't appreciate the comments and pushed him. Prior to their match, they got together a few times to prepare and work some spots. At *WrestleMania XI* in Hartford, LT pinned Bigelow after a flying forearm from the second rope. The match actually turned out pretty well and the major media outlets gave World Wrestling Federation a ton of press coverage.

Bigelow carried the match and since I was at ringside, I helped coach LT from the floor.

Prior to *SummerSlam 1994,* all the fans were concerned about the whereabouts of Undertaker. In January at the *Royal Rumble,* Yokozuna had the help of eight other wrestlers as he locked Undertaker in a casket to win the match. There were some Undertaker sightings, but nobody had seen him for weeks.

"Hey, I am the Million Dollar Man. My money talks and nobody has the ability or resources to bring Undertaker back except me. I will bring him back and he is now guided not by the urn, but by money." Then I brought out a guy who walked, looked, and dressed like Undertaker. But it wasn't him. Eventually the real Undertaker came back, which was a setup for an Undertaker vs. Undertaker match. After throwing the fake Undertaker (Brian Lee— who wrestled as "Prime Time" Brian Lee in Smoky Mountain Wrestling) in a coffin, the real Undertaker won the match and the fake one was never seen again in World Wrestling Federation.

Vince eventually took me out of the announcing booth. He told me that he wanted me exclusively as a manager. Vince wanted me on the road full-time to manage Sid Vicious. I served as his advisor and mentor. I was to groom Sid, and teach him about the business and how to work in the business.

Sid had come into World Wrestling Federation after an incident that had happened overseas with World Championship Wrestling (WCW). He and Arn Anderson got into an altercation at their hotel in England. It led to a fight that ended up with Sid stabbing Arn in the back with a pair of cuticle scissors. After all was said and done, Arn ended up with more than twenty stab wounds. The company fired Sid.

When Vince told me this, I didn't want to do it. The reason was because of my friendship with Arn. I pulled Bruce Prichard to the side and told him, "So, Vince wants me to go on the road and babysit this big and strong yet raw guy who stabbed one of my best friends, Arn, in the back?"

Bruce simply replied, "Yes."

I came to find out that Sid was a decent guy. He wasn't a good technical wrestler, but he had a chiseled body, conducted great interviews, and had respect for the business. He was a legitimate six-nine and was very

Sid Vicious.

intimidating. He listened to me and worked very hard to improve in the ring. He eventually became a two-time World Wrestling Federation Heavyweight Champion.

In 2001 while working for WCW, Sid unfortunately suffered a career-ending injury in the ring. While wrestling Scott Steiner, Sid uncharacteristically went to the middle rope. As he landed, he broke his leg. With the cameras catching every detail, Sid's left leg broke in half, snapping both the fibula and tibia, with one of the bones poking through the skin. It was heartbreaking. What was even more pathetic was how WCW exploited the injury, showing it over and over on TV. I understand Sid is trying to make a comeback and I wish him the best of luck.

While managing Sid, I traveled all over the States and even a couple of times to Europe. I really didn't want to be on the road. It pulled me away from my family. Because of my commitment to the company, and the fact that I needed the money, I sucked it up and went on the road. I thought to myself that everything would eventually work out and my days on the road would soon decrease.

After Sid left the company, I was very fortunate to manage one of the most successful wrestlers in the history of the company, Stone Cold Steve Austin. Back then, he was known as the Ringmaster. Once again, Vince thought that I could help get Steve over with the fans. Steve had worked in the WCW as "Stunning" Steve Austin. He was a good worker and held a few singles titles as well as the tag-team titles with Brian Pillman. Together they were the Hollywood Blondes. While wrestling in Japan, Steve suffered an injury and he had to take some time off. The next thing you know, WCW boss Eric Bischoff fired him. It had also been reported that Eric didn't think Austin was marketable. What was he thinking? Steve would go on to win the World Wrestling Federation Heavyweight Championship on six different occasions and is hands down one of the greatest wrestlers in the history of WWE.

I liked Steve the first time I met him. He was a very likable guy and he had lots of charisma and talent. He had a deep appreciation for the sport and respected those who paved the way for him. Steve was always working to get better and he would always listen to me.

I remember early on, some of the agents were unnecessarily critical of Steve's ring work. Steve asked me, "Ted, so-and-so keeps coming up to me and telling me that I need to do more in the ring, especially my TV matches. They say that I have to pick up the pace and do more high-flying moves and things like that. What do you think?"

"Steve, don't change anything. What you are doing in the ring is wrestling in a way that is believable. You aren't flying all over the ring like a Ping-Pong ball and that's a good thing. Your style makes you different from others. You are wrestling very old-school. Now Steve, the way you work might not get you over with the crowd as fast as the high flyers, but everything you do in the ring is crisp, sound, and believable. And because of your sound technique, you will eventually get over. And when you get over with the crowd, you can bet the house that you will be permanently over. Stick to your guns and keep doing what you are doing in the ring. I believe that you will soon be one of the top heels that this company has ever had." I was right.

Along the way, I gave Steve the Million Dollar Belt. Since he was my guy, it made sense for me to just give him my title. I think the belt and Steve's association with me played a major role in helping him initially get over with the crowd.

I had to face it, my heart was no longer in the wrestling business. Despite all the success I had with World Wrestling Federation from 1987 to 1993 as a wrestler, television commentator, and manager, I no longer wanted to spend so much time on the road. I thought it was time for me to get off the road once and for all, to make my family and faith the top priorities in my life. Since my contract required me to give written notice if I wanted out, I decided to write Vince a letter. The letter was drafted by my attorney to make sure all was legal and per the guidelines of my contract. It said that I did not want to renew my contract as it was written. When Vince received the letter, I guess he was very upset. On May 26, 1996, at the next major Pay-Per-View TV taping, *In Your House 8: Beware of Dog*, Vince said, "Ted, I received your letter. You will finish today."

We shook hands and I said, "Okay, but I really didn't want it to end this way." If Vince had been willing to keep me as a manager and commentator so that I didn't have to be on the road all the time, I would have renegotiated my contract and stayed.

I was told by the creative team that when I went into the ring with Steve, I was to cut this promo. "I am so confident that the Ringmaster can beat Savio Vega that if he doesn't, I will permanently leave World Wrestling Federation forever." In the Caribbean Strap match, I interfered and caused Steve to lose. As I left the ring, the capacity crowd in Florence, South Carolina, were going bananas as they enthusiastically chanted, "Na-na, na-na-na-na, hey, hey, hey, good-bye . . ." After all that I had been through in World Wrestling Federation, it was a pretty unceremonious end to the career of the Million Dollar Man.

The wrestling business had been very good to me. I rose to a level of success and achievement that few guys get to do in the industry. I will always be grateful for the opportunities that Vince gave me with his company. He gave me an unbelievable character and the means to maintain it for nearly a decade. My time with Vince in World Wrestling Federation was hands down the greatest in my career.

I wish I would have spoken to Vince directly and not sent him that letter. At the time, I just didn't think that Vince would understand. I still regret it to this day.

I had a chance to reconcile with Vince in 2003 at Road Warrior Hawk's funeral. Hawk had died in his sleep from a heart attack at forty-six. Along with Nikita Koloff, I was asked to give the eulogy. We were very good friends and I know that before he died he had accepted Jesus as his savior.

During a quiet moment, I pulled Vince aside. It was the first time I had seen him since 1996. We hugged and shook hands, then I said, "Vince, it is great to see you. I haven't had a chance to talk to you in a long time. I just wanted you to know that I shouldn't have sent you that letter. I should have just sat down and told you how I was truly feeling face-to-face. I didn't get a chance to tell you then, but I am telling you now."

Vince nodded his head and said, "You should have told me, Ted. I would have understood. But now I'm glad you told me."

"I got word that you were upset with me because I told some of the boys that I was happy to finally get out of the company. Well, I did make that statement. But it was misinterpreted. It wasn't like, 'Oh my gosh, I am finally out of World Wrestling Federation.' What I was trying to say was that I could finally relax from the grind of being on the road. Please understand that I didn't leave the company because I was dissatisfied or unhappy. I left because I was neglecting my family and trying to get my personal life in order."

"I understand and thank you for sharing that with me."

14

WORLD CHAMPIONSHIP WRESTLING

I wanted to get off the road; however, I still wanted to be part

of the wrestling business. It was in my blood. What else was I sup-

posed to do to make a living? I never graduated from college and had

no other skills. After a show in L.A. back in 1993, I ran into Barry

Bloom, a Hollywood agent who had a number of wrestlers under

contract. Barry and I became friends.

We talked about a lot of things. He sensed that I was unhappy and asked me what was wrong. I poured out my heart to him. I mentioned that I was very unhappy with my current working situation and being away from my family. Barry was supportive and understanding. He mentioned that there might be another option. "They might want you at WCW."

"Really?"

"Sure. Why can't you go to WCW and do the same thing you are doing with Vince? You can go to WCW as a manager or television commentator."

Intrigued, I asked, "Do you think there is any interest?"

"Ted, I don't know but I can easily find out."

I didn't hear from Barry again until we were back on the West Coast for some spot shows. I called Barry and told him I was in town. He told me to swing by the office when I had some time. One afternoon, as I walked into his office, the head of WCW, Eric Bischoff, was there. I didn't stay too long. We exchanged some casual chat and I said, "Okay, guys, I have to leave to get ready for tonight's show." We shook hands and Eric jokingly said, "Ted, if you ever get tired of working where you are, look us up."

A couple of days later, Barry called me and said that WCW had genuine interest in me. It was after the call from Barry that I started thinking about going to work for WCW. I thought that maybe the move would be the best thing for my career and family. Managers in WCW didn't go on the road; I would only have to be away from home every Monday.

In May of 1996, my contract had ended with World Wrestling Federation. According to the provisions, I was required to sit out for ninety days. Meantime, I got ahold of Barry and told him that I was interested in working for WCW. Barry became my agent and he met with Eric Bischoff to negotiate my contract. It was the first time in my wrestling career that I had both an agent and someone else negotiating my contract.

Once the ninety-day clause expired, I signed a six-figure, three-year, stair-stepping, guaranteed no-cut contract with WCW. I would serve as a manager and television commentator. It was substantially more than I had made doing the same thing with World Wrestling Federation. The deal also included first-class round-trip airfare, hotel accommodations, and all my rental car expenses.

I joined the WCW in the middle of World Wrestling Federation vs. WCW. I wasn't alone. I ran into many old World Wrestling Federation wrestlers that Vince had created who had jumped ship: Randy Savage, Hulk Hogan, Kevin Nash, and Scott Hall. It was a landmark time in the wrestling business that no one had experienced before. The greatest angle in wrestling wasn't Hulk Hogan and his newly formed nWo (New World Order) faction, or what was going on in World Wrestling Federation with its New Attitude; it was the war between the two companies. And it was during the advent of hundreds upon hundreds of wrestling websites and 900 telephone numbers, all of them filled with wrestling rumors and information. The fans knew what was going on and they loved it.

Because of the ongoing battle, more people started watching wrestling, more than ever before. Every Monday night, people would switch back and forth between World Wrestling Federation's flagship show, *Raw*, and the WCW's *Nitro*. For a time, more people watched wrestling than *Monday Night Football*.

The Monday Night Wars created some of the best wrestling drama. The talent and writers for both companies pulled out all the stops to attain ratings and sponsors. For more than a year, the WCW was winning the ratings battle. But Vince didn't and never would quit. With the rise of Stone Cold Steve Austin, The Rock, and Mick Foley, WWE eventually won the war.

I was introduced to WCW at a live *Nitro* show. A few weeks prior to me actually being seen on live TV, they showed live clips of the nWo (Hogan, Nash, and Hall) talking to someone in a limousine parked outside the venue. The announcers told the audience and viewers that there was someone in the limo. The viewers couldn't tell who it was. For weeks, they did a good job of building the suspense and teasing the viewers about who it could be.

Finally, the television cameras showed me walking into the arena and taking a seat in the audience. The commentators were stunned and energetically said, "Look at that. Who is it? Oh my gosh, it's Ted DiBiase! What in the world is he doing here on *Nitro*?"

Throughout the two-hour show, they kept cutting to me in the crowd. At the very end of the program, right after the nWo won their match, the camera panned back to me. I was smiling. Then I looked directly in the camera and said, "Next week, four!" As the show concluded, the announcers speculated, "What does Ted DiBiase mean? What does 'Next week, four' mean? What is he talking about?"

The following week on *Nitro*, I came out to the ring with the nWo. I was introduced by Hulk Hogan to the wrestling world not as the Million Dollar Man, but as Billionaire Ted. Vince owned the Million Dollar Man name, but Hogan came up with the nickname. Hogan had used the term quite frequently, though people assumed he was talking about Ted Turner. In October of 1996, when the nWo was beating up the Nasty Boys, Hogan even called me Trillionaire Ted.

Hogan told the crowd that I was the so-called financier behind the nWo. I cut a promo saying, "I am the money and power behind the entire nWo takeover. With my resources and the nWo's power, there is absolutely nothing that anyone can do to stop us!"

VIRGIL:

Ted helped bring me into WCW to serve as the head of security for the nWo. Although they changed my name to Vincent, Teddy and I, along with Hulk Hogan, Kevin Nash, Scott Hall, Syxx, and Eric Bischoff, were the original seven members of the nWo.

The experience was great. I went from one great gimmick as the bodyguard for the Million Dollar Man to the head of security for the hottest faction in professional wrestling, the nWo.

After working a few weeks with the company, I quickly realized that the WCW was one of the most disorganized companies that I had ever been a part of. I sensed that there was an internal power struggle going on among some of the major talent—namely Hulk Hogan, Kevin Nash, and Scott Hall. With all three men having guaranteed contracts, it seemed that each guy was continually battling and jockeying for the spotlight.

Another problem that contributed to the disorganization was that many of the nWo's stars, and other talent, had a creative-control clause in their contract. In other words, if any of the wrestlers didn't want to work with Eric or do what the creative team wanted him to do, then he simply didn't have to do it. It led to no one ever wanting to get beat or lose a match. I can't tell you how much complaining, fighting, and griping went on backstage about who had to win or lose a match. The nWo was very over with the crowd, but because of all the problems, it eventually lost its impact.

The nWo was Eric Bischoff's idea. Although Paul Orndorff and Terry Taylor helped polish up the particulars, Eric deserves credit for the idea. But the nWo was his only idea. What Eric couldn't do was what Vince McMahon could, create stars. Eric didn't have the experience, savvy, or pedigree to do what Vince did with wrestling talent. When Eric was put in charge of WCW, he simply signed a stable of guys, for huge amounts of money, that Vince had already made famous. Unquestionably, Eric Bischoff was no Vince McMahon.

While Paul Orndorff did play a role in the training of Bill Goldberg—at the WCW's Power Plant—Bill was the only wrestler that Eric somewhat developed. Although he had a great look, his wrestling skills were limited. To get Bill over with the crowd, they put him on an unbelievable winning streak: 173 consecutive victories. However, when Kevin Nash beat Goldberg, ending the streak, they didn't know what to do with him.

When I first met Goldberg, we got along. He was nice and a very personable guy. Some guys have told me that Bill let his success go to his head. But he always seemed to have respect for the business. He held numerous titles, including the Heavyweight Championship for about three months back in 1993. Currently retired from wrestling, Bill hosted a reality television series called *Bullrun*, where twelve teams compete in a four-thousand-mile road rally.

My character and role in WCW was affected because of all the internal problems. I was signed by Eric to serve as the manager and mouthpiece of the nWo. As the nWo's popularity started to grow, Eric decided that he wanted to be that mouthpiece. So he took himself out of television commentating and put himself into my role.

I continued to be part of the show and walked into the ring with the nWo, but basically got shelved. It got to the point where I went to Eric and said, "Look, Eric, nothing personal, but I didn't spend twenty-plus years of my life building a name and a career to end up being Hulk Hogan's belt bearer.

The only thing I'm doing is walking to the ring carrying Hogan's belt. In reality, you have taken over my role. Well, it is your company and of course you can do what you want. But if I am not going to play a bigger part in what is going on here, or if you have nothing else for me to do, why don't you just send me home until you figure out what you want to do with me." Eric agreed and sent me home.

Eric Bischoff had some initial success as the head of WCW, but he eventually became a tyrant. He was cocky and brash. He let the success go to his head. I didn't dislike Eric, but I wasn't crazy about him. I saw him as a guy trying to run a big and growing company, but he lacked the background or knowledge to do so. He also spent way too much money on his number one objective: putting Vince McMahon out of business.

One night after a show, in which we tore the house down and had record attendance, Eric said, "I'm going to put Vince out of business."

"Eric, that will never happen. Vince might retreat to the East Coast or downsize, but let me tell you something, he is never going away. Wrestling is in his blood and it is a part of who he is and his life. He will fight tooth and nail to win." I could tell Eric was angered by my comments. The grinding of his teeth and facial expressions told me that he didn't want to hear what I had to say. Yet, I continued, "Eric, I can assure you of this, and I will say it one more time, Vince is not going away."

Eventually, Vince McMahon won the Monday Night Wars and he bought WCW. Vince now controls the largest wrestling company in the world. Eric Bischoff, who vowed to put Vince out of business, soon became an employee of his. He served as the general manager of *Raw*. I'm sure Eric had to eat a lot of crow.

I got paid to do absolutely nothing for two years. I just sat at home and watched the checks come in the mail every two weeks. Eric sent me out a couple of times to make appearances. One time, he sent me out to promote the nWo's NASCAR race car. I went to the track to commentate and cover the race. The WCW sponsored the nWo car that raced in the Busch Series. For a while, the driver of the car was Kyle Petty, son of NASCAR legend Richard Petty.

I also did color commentating one time at a Pay-Per-View with Eric in

Des Moines. When I commentated with World Wrestling Federation, I thoroughly prepared for the event, and all the announcers had notes. I can recall going to a two-hour live taping of *Nitro*. As the show was about to go on the air, they still had no idea what they were going to do at the end of the night. At that Pay-Per-View, nothing had changed; Eric and I didn't prepare and it showed. Without any notes or practice takes, we winged the whole show. We were both color commentators and kept overlapping and cutting each other off. We missed cues and messed up names. In short, we totally stunk!

BOBBY "THE BRAIN" HEENAN:

WCW wasn't really a wrestling company. It was one of the many television programs that Ted Turner had on his network. Turner made a lot of money and cut big deals, but he couldn't run a TV station by himself. So he hired people to run the various stations, such as the Cartoon Network, CNN, TBS, which aired the Atlanta Hawks and the Atlanta Braves games, et cetera. He put people in charge of WCW that didn't know how to run a wrestling show and draw money. He didn't hire any wrestling people. Eric Bischoff isn't a wrestling person. Vince Russo even tried to bring in Hollywood actors and have them wrestle. There were seven to fourteen different writers and bookers while I was there. Nobody knew each other, nobody knew what was going on, and nobody cared. It wasn't run professionally.

There were too many bosses and nobody knew what to do. There was one lady who worked in production that was a total idiot and I have no idea how she was ever involved in the television industry. She couldn't even properly put a staple on a piece of paper. And you wonder why the company went under?

We were doing 7 and 8 in the ratings, whereas the Braves were only doing a 1. Turner didn't want the public to know that wrestling was doing a major portion of their network's business. If Turner wanted to, he could have put us on CNN or do anything he wanted with the company. Yes, they were doing excellent in the ratings for more than a year. But that didn't necessarily mean they were good. It just meant they were lucky.

While I was at home, my faith in God was growing. I was asked by several organizations and churches to make appearances and give presentations. They wanted me to share my experiences. In November of 1996, I appeared on *The 700 Club*, the news talk show of the Christian Broadcasting Network (CBN), hosted by the Reverend Pat Robertson. We had a great discussion about my life, the wrestling business, and my salvation. Near the end of the interview I said to Pat, "Fans ask me all the time about which was my toughest match."

"What was your answer?"

"I tell them that my toughest match was with God."

"Did God pin you?"

"No, Pat, I gave up."

Since I was getting paid for doing nothing for WCW, I came up with an idea. I contacted Eric. "Wrestling fans aren't stupid. With the hundreds of wrestling websites that are pumping out information about the business by the hour, as well as 900 hotlines, I think it would be best if you turned me babyface. Since I am a Christian, it doesn't make sense for me to be a heel."

Eric replied, "Ted, you're right. Let's do it."

Eric brought me back on TV as a babyface manager for the Steiner Brothers and Ray Traylor. Although it didn't make sense, I turned face by way of an interview. It also didn't make sense to have me manage the Steiners or Ray. Scott and Ric didn't need a manager, nor did Ray. Neither of these angles ended up going anywhere, so I eventually ended up back home doing nothing but collecting my check.

When I was managing the Steiners, I was sitting by myself in the dining room of the Marriott hotel in Atlanta. I looked into the lounge area and saw many of the guys drinking and flirting with the ladies. For the first time, I saw the game in which I had been a major player. I thought to myself, "Man, that used to be me. What was I thinking? How stupid was I?"

Because of all of WCW's disorganization and incompetence, my desire for the business dwindled. My life had changed and my focus was now clearly on my family and my faith. I wanted to be on the road sharing my testimony rather than in the wrestling ring. I enjoyed going to various high schools throughout the country and talking to kids about the dangers of alcohol and drug abuse.

Over the last decade, I have seen many of my friends in the wrestling business die. Guys like Terry Gordy, Rick Rude, Big Boss Man, Bam Bam Bigelow, JYD, Road Warrior Hawk, Brian Pillman, Hercules Hernandez, Miss Elizabeth, Kerry Von Erich, and Louie Spicolli.

Kerry Von Erich was a great guy and everybody loved him, including me. He had a great heart and had a tremendous respect for the business. He was a second-generation wrestler and the son of Fritz Von Erich. He and his four brothers were icons in the state of Texas. The female fans simply adored him. He held numerous titles, including the NWA Heavyweight Championship and the World Wrestling Federation Intercontinental title.

I believe Kerry was also addicted to drugs. He started by getting hooked on painkillers, then mixing them with alcohol. As he was riding his motorcycle, he got into an accident and his right foot was severed. Amazingly, Kerry continued to wrestle. The pain was obviously unbearable and he was eventually arrested for writing prescriptions for himself. For twenty-something years, the Dallas–Fort Worth police let Kerry off because of his name. He should have been sent for counseling, but the justice system had him pay a fine and placed him on probation. It all came to an end when he was arrested in 1993 at his apartment for possession of cocaine. Since he was on probation, he was going to spend time in a federal prison. He was upset about having to serve jail time. After being released on bond, Kerry went out to his father's property. He took a .44 magnum, placed it over his heart, and pulled the trigger. I miss my friend Kerry.

Louie Spicolli is another guy who I got to know when we worked together in WCW. At the time, he wasn't used that much by the creative team, but he was starting to get a push. One night after a *Nitro* show in Macon, I drove back to Atlanta to spend the night at the Airport Marriott. While eating in the hotel restaurant, Louie asked to join me. He had a beer in each hand. After about thirty minutes, his speech started to become slurred. I said, "Louie, are you okay?"

"Yeah, I'm fine." The next thing you know, Louie was passed out right at the table. Along with some help, I took Louie up to his room.

At the show the next day, I saw Louie. I went up to him. "Louie, can I share something with you?"

"Sure."

"It's none of my business and you can do whatever you want to do, but I know you are taking sleeping pills. But if you don't stop, you'll end up being one of those guys we read about in the paper. It may not be tomorrow, next month, or even next year. But somewhere down the road it will all come to an end. If you want me to help you or get you some help, please tell me."

"I'm okay, Ted. I'm not that bad. I don't do it all the time. I have it all under control."

"You know what, Louie, that is what all those who are now dead used to say!"

About a month or so later, Louie was a no-show at a *Nitro* event. The next day I got a phone call from one of the boys telling me that Louie had died. They found him in his Los Angeles apartment. He had overdosed on Somas and had drowned in his own vomit.

After my contract with WCW expired in 1999, I retired from wrestling. It was time that I focused full-time on my family and ministry. For the last three years, I'd felt a calling to share my testimony with others. I traveled throughout the country and Canada to help other people overcome their demons and lead them to eternal life through the blood of Jesus. For the next five years, I spent all my time and energy with my family and ministry.

15

CORPORATE MAN

The family and I were now living in Clinton, Mississippi. It was the perfect location for us, with Melanie's parents living ten minutes down the road. For the past six years, I was enjoying my life as a minister and watching Brett and Teddy grow up. Both boys were very athletic and I really enjoyed going to Brett's high school soccer games. But in December of 2004, I received a phone call from Arn Anderson that once again led me back to WWE.

Arn's call was from out of the blue. I'd had zero communication with anyone regarding my return to professional wrestling. I hadn't heard from him since my final days in WCW. Arn and I are very good friends. I have known him since my days in Bill Watts's Mid-South territory. He was a great worker and, like me, retired from wrestling in the late 1990s because of extensive neck and upper back injuries. He is most famous in wrestling for his role as the enforcer with the legendary Four Horsemen. Arn is now a producer for WWE.

After exchanging pleasantries, we talked about the current state of WWE. He said, "John Laurinaitis [the director of talent relations for WWE], Michael Hayes, and others in the company brought your name up and wanted me to give you a call."

"Sure, what's up?"

"Teddy, WWE wants to know if you are interested in coming back to work for the company in a creative capacity. In other words, to be a part of the creative team and help to lay out the game plan for the wrestlers."

I was silent. To say I was shocked would be an understatement. Then I replied, "Arn, aren't they aware that because of my faith I've spoken out against some of the WWE programming—too much flesh, sexual innuendos, and violence. I can't believe that they would think I have any interest."

Arn added, "They know how you feel and respect your opinion. Because of your work in the ministry, do you think that you would still be interested in working in this capacity?"

"I'm not sure."

"Well, are you at least willing to talk to John?"

"Yeah, sure. Have him give me a call."

ARN ANDERSON:

I first met Teddy while working for Bill Watts in the old Mid-South territory. I had just started in the business. Teddy took an interest in me and we became friends. Although he was one of the top performers in the territory, he still took time out of his schedule to watch my matches. He really helped me in the early days of my career. I'll never forget it. When I left the territory, I reminded Teddy that if there ever was an opportunity when I could repay him for helping me, I would.

Although it took nearly two decades, in late 2004, a road agent and creative team opportunity became available in WWE. I was working in the same capacity. Granted, there are many talented people who work in creative from outside the business, but you also need guys who are from the inside. We needed someone who had drawn money and knew how the business worked. The first person that came to mind for the opening was Teddy. He had the experience and conducted himself in a professional manner. It was a no-brainer.

So I called Teddy. We had a good conversation. I then asked him if he wanted to work for the company. He eventually did and it was a great hire for WWE.

MICHAEL HAYES:

I really pushed for Teddy to be part of the creative team. Since the wrestling business has evolved, many of the talents don't have the benefit and the experience of coming up through the territorial system. In hindsight, this is probably a detractor right now for the industry because the territories were the place where talent could hone and learn their craft. Thus, when they got to the big show, they were experienced veterans and knew what to do to get over and how to perform on top. This isn't the case today.

As the company grew, it was brought up to me on many occasions that if there was anyone out there that had a really good mind for the business, loved the business, and could help teach, then I should try to get that person on board. Teddy's name was at the forefront of my mind, and the office reached out to him because of his immense qualifications and ability to satisfy our guidelines.

After a few days, I spoke with John. He repeated what Arn had told me. "If you come back to work for WWE, you would report directly to Stephanie McMahon. If you are interested, we will make all the arrangements to fly you up here to interview with her." After discussing it over with Melanie, I agreed.

I missed the wrestling business. It was the only thing that I really knew. Melanie and I both agreed that I should at least listen to what the company had to say.

In January of 2005, I flew to New York. It was déjà vu. A limo picked me up at the airport and took me to the WWE main offices in Stamford. Just like in 1987, the same concerns and questions were racing through my head.

I immediately met with Stephanie. We hugged and shared some laughs. She was very gracious and conducted herself as a consummate professional. I found it ironic. The person that might be my boss was the same person I watched grow up in the business. I've always liked Stephanie. As most people know, she is the daughter of WWE chairman Vince McMahon and Linda McMahon and is married to Triple H. She works for the company as the executive vice president of creative writing and is the head of the creative team. She's a graduate of Boston University and is one of the most articulate individuals I've ever met.

During the interview, Stephanie explained the position. "Ted, because of your in-ring experience and success, we are interested in bringing you back to serve as an advisor to the creative team writers. These are the folks who write the story lines for the shows. We will also have you do some work as a producer, where you will help the wrestlers work out their matches for *SmackDown!*"

"Stephanie, that's great. I am very interested, but as you know, I've been a critic of some of your programming, such as the Stone Cold Steve Austin character. He is a great guy, but I have a problem with what his character projects. He comes to the ring flipping people off, drinking beer like it's water, and cursing like a sailor. You have young kids in the audience and I think it's very inappropriate. Stephanie, one of these days you will have a child. When the two of you are watching wrestling, do you want his hero to be a stone cold, beer-guzzling bully?"

"I'm aware of your concern and you are entitled to your opinion. But

Ted, things have changed. Everything today is driven by ratings. We have to answer to our sponsors and their bottom line is all about ratings. Regarding Steve, I see your point, but Ted, we didn't make Steve a babyface, the fans did."

The moral decay of our society is something that we all need to be concerned about. I don't agree with all the trashy lyrics in rap music and the near obscene music videos. Don't get me wrong, I support free speech. But there have to be some limits on certain types of speech, especially when it infringes upon others and violates the basic moral codes of this great nation. Let's forget the fact that I am a minister, but as a man, I believe that something has to be done to protect our children from the profanity and sex-driven advertising. There is a clear difference between what is right and what is wrong. Just because one can doesn't mean that they should.

Stephanie and I chatted about the position some more. "I am willing to give it a try, but to be perfectly honest, I may not be cut out for it. I am comfortable working as a producer, where I can coach talent based on what I have acquired and learned over the years. As far as being an advisor and script writer, however, I'm not so sure."

"Ted, we are not asking you to be a writer. We are asking you to listen to what the writers are scripting and then put that in a wrestling perspective."

"Okay, perhaps I can do that. I am very interested and I will give it some thought."

Stephanie concluded the interview by telling me that she was going to interview some other people and would get back to me in a few days. She told me that her brother Shane was down the hall and wanted to see me. Like I did with Stephanie, I watched Shane grow up in the business. He's a great guy and we shared a few laughs. Shane works as a vice president for the company and sometimes wrestles. He can do some incredible aerial moves in the ring. As Shane walked me to the limo, I spoke to a few other folks. It was very therapeutic to see many old acquaintances.

Before leaving, I spoke to Jim Ross. I have known Jim since my Mid-South days and we are good friends. He is the lead announcer for WWE and is, bar none, the best wrestling announcer ever to call a match. I closed the door behind Jim and explained to him my concerns about the position. He understood and bluntly said, "Ted, this is a job that will keep you up at night. You're constantly thinking about what to do, where the angle can go, what will happen with it in the long term. I know that if you really want to do the job, and your heart is in it, you will succeed. But keep in mind, you have to really want to do it."

As I headed to the airport, I had mixed feelings about the position. I was very happy serving in my current position as a preacher and spreading the word of God throughout my ministry. On the other hand, I was not the Million Dollar Man in real life. The pay of a preacher is nominal. The position would offer a better salary and a great benefits package. It would also allow me the opportunity to continue preaching on my off days. I was intrigued by the opportunity. I had done almost everything in the wrestling business. The position would now allow me to have done it all in professional wrestling.

I will always have a place in my heart for the wrestling business. Despite the grind and temptations of the road, I guess my love for the business is why I kept going back into wrestling over and over again. It had been an integral part of my life; once it's in your blood, you never lose the desire to be a part of the industry.

While waiting for my flight home to Jackson, I made a few calls. I told Melanie about the interview and my reservations. She was very supportive and reminded me, "Teddy, you have the credentials to do a great job. You were one of the best wrestlers ever in WWE. If you really want to do it, you can." She boosted me up some more and told me not to sell myself short. I needed to hear that because for whatever reason, I sometimes have a problem with self-confidence.

I also called Shawn Michaels. Shawn and I are very close friends. Our friendship goes back to when he broke into the business in the Mid-South territory. I remember the first time I saw him in the dressing room. He was very young and had a real baby face. He was extremely quiet and respected the veterans in the room. He watched and learned from those who were in the ring. Over the years, I have watched the Heartbreak Kid grow in the business from a tag-team wrestler to one of the greatest workers in the history of our profession.

In the prime of my wrestling career in World Wrestling Federation,

Shawn and I would regularly drink beer and chat about the business. We wrestled on the same cards together throughout the country. Because of our interaction, we became good friends. He would often get frustrated because he felt the company wasn't utilizing his talents. After one of his vent sessions I told him, "Shawn, there is one thing that this business will never deny and that is talent. The cream will always rise to the top. You are talented and your time will come. There are all types of politics involved in this business. Sooner or later you will get your shot. Believe me, don't give up and keep going. Your time will come."

SHAWN MICHAELS:

I met Teddy in the Mid-South territory, which was where I first broke into the business. He was the top heel. I didn't talk too much back then and kept to myself, respecting the veterans. During that time, I was a jobber and got beat up a lot. But I will never forget the match I had on TV against Ted. I only did two moves—a sunset flip and a small package. But Teddy worked the match in such a way that it was probably the best match for my career in the territory. Ted gave me so much feedback and helped me to understand why things were to be done in the ring. For me at such an early stage of my career to have someone like Teddy take time out to teach me speaks volumes about him.

I shared my heart with Shawn and told him my concerns about the position with the company. "Shawn, I just don't know about this opportunity. There is a part of me that says I can do it and another part that says I'm not cut out for it."

"Ted, you have to follow your heart. I think you can do it. Just keep in mind, however, it is a very demanding position. The folks on the creative team work more than people give them credit for. You know I would love to have you working here. Just pray about it. I am sure you will make the correct decision."

SHAWN MICHAELS:

I supported Teddy being part of the creative team and a producer. To work in those capacities, Teddy had to try to teach a generation that simply didn't have an appreciation for the business. It was hard for him to find a connection with the talent. I think he also felt the business had changed.

He felt that everything that he was good at, perhaps, did not apply. And that really wasn't true. To me, that is why he never got comfortable in those positions. He believed it had changed, and in fact it hadn't. All the basics that he knew so well and could do so well were just tough for him to relay to the younger generation. Teddy took that as a failure on his part, but really it was a failure of the generation to appreciate the basics and foundations that will always be a part of professional wrestling.

At thirty thousand feet, my mind continued to explore. Although Stephanie had told me that I would be on the road four days a week and home the other three, I began to wonder if I could be away from my family for even that duration. I had enjoyed spending time, for the past six years, with Melanie and the boys. I wasn't quite sure that I wanted to break the continuity.

By now, my two oldest boys were interested in becoming professional wrestlers. Although I wished they wouldn't pursue that career route, I was supportive of their desires. Melanie told me that if they offered me the position, and I accepted, it would be a great opportunity to be with my boys in the business. I could be there to watch over them and help influence and guide their careers. It all made sense, and the pros outweighed the cons. I made the decision that if they offered me the position, I would accept.

About two weeks passed and I hadn't heard anything. I started to wonder if they had chosen someone else. Then one day in early March, I received a phone call in my office while I was preparing for an upcoming speech to the Promise Keepers. It was Stephanie. "Ted, we decided to choose you for the advisor to the creative team position. If you are still interested, we would love to have you be part of our company."

Without hesitation, I said, "Yes!"

We talked about the work schedule and some of my other prior commitments. Stephanie understood and knew I had to honor them. We settled on a starting date of April 6, 2005, three days after *WrestleMania XXI* in Los Angeles. Meantime, Stephanie gave me my first assignment: to start watching the wrestling matches on TV and familiarize myself with the WWE characters.

As I watched the shows on TV, everything seemed so foreign. It was like watching a different business. It was more entertainment than when I was wrestling. I watched a two-hour show and only saw four or five matches. It wasn't a wrestling show anymore. There was a lot more drama and scripted talking.

The one thing that stood out was the talent; they all looked the same. Everybody was built like a muscle head. They had tattoos all over their bodies and had bald heads. I wondered what had happened to all the characters in the business. In the 1980s, Vince McMahon created characters like the Million Dollar Man, Koko B. Ware, Brutus "The Barber" Beefcake, the Bushwhackers, Randy "Macho Man" Savage, Yokozuna, I.R.S., Undertaker, and Hulk Hogan. Everybody was different. But now, everybody looked the same. It was too much of the same thing. New characters were needed.

When I reported it to the creative team, they concurred with my observation. The creative team was comprised of some very bright people. They were all young college graduates who had some experience in Hollywood script writing. The writers were wrestling fans and very energetic.

The wrestling industry had changed and WWE was not a wrestling company anymore. It was a sports entertainment company. The writers are needed to create the best product on the planet. You could tell that they really loved the business. A couple of them just amazed me because they knew all my matches, specific dates, and other things about my career that I had long forgotten.

However, you still need people in the business to help polish up the wrestling side. The creative script writers knew how to write and put stories together, but they didn't know the nuts and bolts of wrestling. They had never been in the ring, and only those who had been in the ring could truly appreciate and understand a wrestling match. This is why producers are needed to help put together the matches.

I noticed that there was definitely a difference in the level of talent within the company. Besides the top guys—Triple H, Shawn Michaels, Ric Flair, Undertaker, and Eddie Guerrero—the others didn't have the same level of believability. The success of professional wrestling is based on believability. Although the fans know it is staged, the talent still has to be able to make it seem as real as possible, to tell a story, to make people want to watch and follow the angle. The talent roster was weak.

The producers had to map out matches from bell to bell. It's not because the talent was bad, but because they hadn't been trained to be in-ring generals. Years ago, the talent would learn the craft by going from territory to territory. Today, there is nowhere for the talent to learn. To help with this shortcoming, WWE created developmental territories, one in Florida and another in Ohio. This is where wrestlers learn their craft from trainers like Steve Keirn and "Dr. Death" Steve Williams. But when they are called up to the big leagues, many are still raw and inexperienced, and the producers have to help them organize their matches.

John Cena is a talent who has dramatically improved over a short period of time. He is a product of WWE's Ohio Valley developmental territory. I give John a tremendous amount of credit. He is an excellent athlete and an overall great person. When you are the champion, Vince runs you hard. Besides doing the wrestling matches and interviews, the champ also is the company's chief spokesperson. There are media appearances, charity events, community activities—the list goes on and on. The champ is required to do whatever Vince asks of him, to help promote and market WWE.

I used to see John every day and we chatted quite frequently. "Hey, champ, how are you holding up, buddy?"

"I am doing okay."

I continued, "Listen, you have to look at it like this: if you keep it up at this pace, you won't have to worry about anything too much longer. You will be financially set for life."

With a big grin, John smiled and said, "Ted, that's the plan."

I enjoyed working as a producer a lot more than being part of the creative team. Although Dusty Rhodes and Michael Hayes are good friends, and we had fun working together on the creative team, I was more comfortable being close to the in-ring action. For example, at *WrestleMania 22* in Chicago, I was in charge of the Hardcore match between Mick Foley and Edge. It isn't difficult to script a match when you are working with two great talents. I just listened to what they had to say as they laid out their match. They knew exactly what they wanted to do and it made sense. After working for a very exciting fifteen minutes, Edge defeated Mick after spearing him off the apron and through a flaming table outside the ring.

After a couple of months on the job, I knew it was something I couldn't do. The reason being that I never did it. The art of wrestling is improvising. If one is really good at what he does, he does it instinctively. It is the main reason why I eventually failed in my position as a producer.

I also failed as an advisor to the creative team. I think creative writing is a gift. Throughout my entire wrestling career, I never came up with my own gimmicks. Guys like Bill Watts and Vince McMahon gave me my character. I was the actor. If someone told me what he wanted, I could make it happen in the ring and do it instinctively. I couldn't become someone else's character and help him put together his game plan.

ARN ANDERSON:

Teddy was a great performer and he wrestled on instinct and feel. He acted, reacted, and adjusted to the situation in the ring. He was an excellent worker and an in-ring general. He was always a gentleman and very knowledgeable. He was diverse in the ring and is probably one of the top twenty-five performers of all time.

Even though Teddy performed in the ring at the highest level, it didn't necessarily mean that he could picture that and translate it to someone else. We work in a very specialized field. There are only a few people in the world who have an aptitude for this aspect of the business. Today, we have guys in the business who need lots of guidance, preparation, and training. Teddy wasn't able to translate what he knew to the workers. It just didn't work out. I didn't consider it a failure. Rather, I think Teddy just got frustrated. Not everyone can be a producer. It doesn't demean who he is, or what he has meant to the business.

STEVE KEIRN:

When Teddy came in as a producer, I don't think he ever had any experience teaching anyone else in this business. He never taught or passed his trade on to anyone. Teddy was undoubtedly one of the greatest workers in the history of wrestling and could do anything in the ring. To turn around and explain how he did it, and how you could do what he did, was something that Teddy had never had experience in. He was put in a position where his job was to make the talent better. Teddy could see the mistakes, but he didn't have the descriptive analysis to teach people that made those mistakes how not to make them again. He fumbled with this and eventually started to feel insecure. So he was man enough to admit not only to himself but to everyone else that he just wasn't getting the job done.

MICHAEL HAYES:

Was Teddy born to be on the creative team? No. He was very creative in the ring during his career as a wrestler, but trying to communicate with kids today isn't the same as in Teddy's era. Being a producer is something that takes a lot of patience and it just didn't come easy for him. He is not alone. The position is a never-ending job and there is never a finish line. Consequently, you never have any time to enjoy the success of victory.

Teddy also has that low voice, which at times was a hindrance when communicating with the production crew and getting the information to them in enough time. We always try to give the folks in the production truck a heads-up as to what is going to happen in the ring. We want to give them at least thirty to sixty seconds to get ready for a spot so they can have time to get their cameras in place. I think for the old-school guys like Teddy, it was hard to make the transition from the ring to calling the matches (it took me a long time to learn). In his matches and back in the old days, you just called your spots and did your moves as they happened. In today's television world, that doesn't give the camera operators and directors time to get ready for whatever is going to happen. Teddy just couldn't make the transition.

I don't know that Teddy was totally unsuccessful. I think he did have some victories. There is no doubt that he definitely improved from the time he got there to when he left the creative team. Teddy is used to succeeding. He never just passed at anything he had ever done. He wasn't doing A work but C work. Teddy doesn't like average. He certainly tried and gave it all he had. The job just isn't meant for everybody.

MIKE ROTUNDO (I.R.S.):

I had just started out as a producer when Ted left the company. From talking with him, I think Ted just wasn't comfortable working as a producer. It is an ever-changing and difficult job. You have to be able to translate to the talent what the creative team and production office wants.

Although Ted was uneasy in that capacity, he was probably one of the greatest wrestlers in the history of the business. He also has a big heart and I really enjoyed my time being around him.

I accepted my shortcomings and tried my best. I valued the company and appreciated the opportunity and the challenge. I was so frustrated that on a flight with Vince McMahon I shared my genuine concern and feelings. Vince listened and encouraged me to stick with it. "Ted, you remind me a lot of Ray Stevens."

"What do you mean?"

"Ray was one of the greatest workers in the wrestling business. But when I asked him why he did what he did in the ring, he couldn't tell me."

"Vince, you are absolutely right."

For the next ten months, I continued serving as an advisor and producer. I had a few cameo appearances at some shows and was even part of the huge Legends Homecoming ceremony in Dallas. One day at a TV taping of *SmackDown!*, Stephanie called me into the office. I sensed by her teary eyes and tone that something was up. "Well, Ted, we gave you a chance as an advisor but things don't seem to be working out." She lightheartedly added, "I guess you were right, Ted. This advising to the creative team isn't your forte." We laughed. "But I spoke to Johnny and we are going to keep you on full-time as a producer." I thanked Stephanie and deep down was quite relieved.

In December of 2005, I was stressed out. The pressure was tremendous. It had been a grueling year for me because I felt I wasn't getting the job done. I felt like a stranger in a very familiar place. But I pressed on to perform well for the company.

JIM ROSS:

I think it would be challenging and not necessarily accurate for anyone to say that Ted's tenure as a producer in WWE could be termed a "failure." There was never a lack of effort or hard work on Ted's behalf that I ever witnessed or heard anyone speak of. I do remember talking to Ted while he was on his visit to WWE to interview for the position. I could tell that he wasn't sure that the job or role was going to fit him personally, but he seemed like he wanted to try it nonetheless. I told him that day in my office that coming back into the business full-time after such a long absence was going to be extremely challenging.

The product had changed in many ways since he was last

earning a living in wrestling and it was far from being a good old boys' club any longer. The corporate world presents many challenges to old-school guys such as Ted DiBiase and so many others I could name, including me. Ted has a wealth of knowledge regarding the business but the job simply wasn't for him. If one isn't able to make the all-important emotional investment in any role within sports entertainment, the chances of long-term success are fleeting.

Ted had all the right intentions when he first started the job with WWE. But one could tell after several weeks that his heart just wasn't in it, even after he left the creative team and returned to his roots on the road as a producer. Although Ted's stay on the road was relatively short, I would still bet a barbecue dinner that many WWE competitors learned a great deal from him. His calming demeanor was a breath of fresh air in the somewhat manic world of sports entertainment.

For that year, I neglected my health. I didn't exercise, nor watch what I was eating. My weight ballooned to over three hundred pounds. The more nervous and stressed-out I got, the more I ate. I was living four days a week at a hotel and eating out three or four times a day, sometimes very late at night.

One morning as I was getting dressed at the hotel, I started feeling very light-headed. I broke out in a cold sweat. I looked into the bathroom mirror and saw that my face was pale. I started to take deep breaths. The next thing I recall was lying on the bathroom floor with my head jacked up against the wall. I had passed out. I was really scared. The first thing I did was grab ahold of my left arm and then my chest to see if I had had a heart attack. Nothing hurt and everything seemed to be fine. I shrugged it off and sat down on the bed to gather my faculties. Everything seemed to be all right.

After getting dressed, I telephoned Dusty Rhodes. "Dream, I just passed out."

He said, "What? Do you want me to come to your room?"

"No, I'm okay now. I'll meet you down in the restaurant in about ten minutes."

Dusty replied, "Are you sure?"

"Yes, don't worry. I'll be right down."

Dusty was waiting for me at the restaurant and he was very concerned. I told him that everything was okay and we went ahead and ordered breakfast. I wasn't too hungry so I only ordered coffee. From what I've been told, after taking a sip of the coffee, I looked straight up at Dusty, my eyes rolled into the back of my head, and I fell right off the chair, landing on the floor. I had passed out again.

When I came to that time, my head was in Dusty's lap. He was on the floor with me. I was very afraid and concerned. Dusty was encouraging me and said, "Don't worry about anything, brother, you are going to be okay. We are going to get you out of here and take you to the hospital." With Dusty by my side, I was transported by the hotel van to the local hospital in Stamford.

Once I got to the emergency room, they quickly admitted me and checked my vitals. Everything appeared to be fine. I spent the rest of the day undergoing a series of tests. I was poked and prodded for what seemed like an eternity. They ran blood tests and a stress test, scanned my brain, and took X-rays. The good news was that after spending all day in the hospital, they couldn't find anything wrong. My heart and brain were fine. The doctor did have one concern: my weight. I weighed in at a whopping 326 pounds. They decided to keep me overnight. I took a fasting blood-sugar test. The results showed that my blood sugar was fluctuating, and that was why I passed out.

I was relieved they were able to diagnose the problem. But I was also afraid: the doctor said that if I didn't get my weight down I could become a diabetic. Before being released, I was given some medicine and put on a strict diet that cut out concentrated sugars. I was also advised to get back into the gym and exercise. So I did. Since then, I haven't had any other health problems.

After taking a few weeks off, I continued working exclusively as a producer. I began to like the producer position. Although I would miss working with Dusty Rhodes and Michael Hayes in the office, it felt good to have less responsibility. I also was working with some great guys like Arn Anderson, Ricky Steamboat, Steve Keirn, and Dave Finlay.

There were many times when Vince would get upset at the shows. He is so passionate for the business and puts all his energy and time into making the show the best it can be. I will never forget the night when Ricky and I were in charge of planning the Undertaker and Muhammad Hassan match. It was a supershoot—two live hours of *Raw,* two taped hours of *SmackDown!* in one night. It was total madness with nonstop action. While going over the match, Undertaker decided that he didn't want to chokeslam Hassan's manager, Daivari. He felt that the two were going to be beaten up so much that the chokeslam wasn't needed. It was my job to report back to Vince and tell him about the match. To the best of my recollection, I told Vince that Undertaker did not want to do a chokeslam and Vince said that it was all right.

As the match concluded, I was standing next to Vince in the gorilla position. All of a sudden Vince went nuts and started screaming, "Where is my chokeslam? Where in the fuck is my damn chokeslam!?" The match ended in front of a live crowd without a chokeslam. Vince was losing it and screaming into the microphone at the referee, "Tell Undertaker to get his ass back in the ring and give Daivari a chokeslam." The message was relayed and he did it. Although the ending seemed awkward to the live audience, the mishap was easily edited, like nothing had happened, for the taped *SmackDown!* national television viewing audience.

Ricky and I had left the gorilla position to go critique the match with Undertaker and Hassan/Daivari. But Vince was still steaming. He screamed from the gorilla position, "Where is the producer of that match?" He looked over at me and Ricky and motioned for us to come over to him. "Ricky, where was my damn chokeslam?"

Ricky replied, "Well, Undertaker didn't want to do it. He didn't think it was needed nor made sense."

Vince replied in a coy manner, "Undertaker didn't want to do it? This is my fucking company and you tell Undertaker he had better do what I say! I am the only one that makes changes to the script!" He continued, giving Ricky a major butt chewing. The entire time I just stood there, doing and saying nothing. I was almost certain that Vince knew of and approved of the change. I felt bad for Ricky and asked him if he wanted me to talk to Vince. Ricky wisely said, "Teddy, let's just go ahead and let this one go. There is no need to bring it back up."

At production meetings, Vince was a stickler about people having their cell phones turned off. Invariably, guys would forget to turn them off or put them on vibrate. While Vince was leading a meeting, someone would telephone the producers to see if their cell phones would ring. Like clockwork, someone's phone would ring and Vince would give them this stare.

On October 25, 2006, one day after doing TV in St. Louis, I was released from WWE. John Laurinaitis called me up at home and said, "Ted, I'm sorry but things aren't working out. I know you've struggled with the position. We are also making some changes so we are going to have to release you."

"I fully understand and have appreciated the opportunity."

There were no hard feelings and I have nothing negative to say about anyone in WWE Corporate. They gave me ample opportunities to improve and learn the two positions. It just didn't work out. In a way, I was actually relieved. I knew that I wasn't doing a good job for the company. The business that I knew and loved wasn't the same business that I was trying to produce. Although the basic fundamentals are still there, the bottom line was entertainment. I am and will always be a wrestler who entertained, not an entertainer who wrestled.

16
MINISTER TED

I am often asked how someone goes from an athlete and professional wrestler to a minister. I can categorically say that I just didn't wake up one morning and think I had this great idea to preach. Growing up, I had always believed in God. My faith had always been strong and helped carry me through many adversities in my life, such as the untimely death of my father and my mother's alcoholism. My belief in God gives me the strength to continue with life despite all the tragedies in it. Also, my transformation from the ring to the pulpit started when I was still a part of World Wrestling Federation.

In 1992, I was at the top my game. I had money and fame and was climbing the ladder of success. I had a loving wife and a great family. But deep down, there was a void in my life. I had been consumed with ego and pride. Like some rock 'n' roll stars, professional athletes, movie stars, and politicians, I engaged in many immature and youthful indiscretions, such as infidelity. On the outside, it looked like I had everything. But deep down, there was something missing.

At *WrestleMania VIII* in Indianapolis, the Natural Disasters (Tugboat & Earthquake) beat I.R.S. and me (Money Inc.) via disqualification. We intentionally got ourselves counted out and thus retained the tag-team titles. I had stayed out all night with the boys, enjoying myself. When I arrived at the hotel in the wee hours of the morning, I called Melanie to check in. The conversation was less than cordial. Melanie was crying. She confronted me about my infidelity. I couldn't believe it. I swallowed hard and apologized. "Melanie, I'm so sorry. I don't want to talk about it over the phone. I'll cancel my trip and immediately come home."

"No, Ted, you won't. You don't live here anymore!" Then she hung up the phone.

For days, I was overwhelmed with the thought that I had lost everything. I wasn't concerned about my material possessions. Rather, I was scared about losing my wife and family. Due to my immaturity, I had disgraced the most important person in my life. Melanie is the woman that I love. She is the mother of my two children. She even accepted my son from a previous marriage, Michael, as her own. I also put at risk the stability and well-being of my children. For what? To pretty much be a self-serving jerk. All I was doing was being unfaithful to my wife while serving my ego.

For days I agonized over what to do. I left the tour early and sought guidance from my pastor and best friend to this day, Hal Santos. He had helped comfort Melanie and even worked to get us back together. I confessed and accepted Jesus in my heart. I asked the Lord to guide me and I promised to change.

With Hal's help, I realized that for Melanie to take me back, I had to be truly sorry and willing to change. I had to prove to her that my days of drinking, experimenting with drugs, and chasing women were over. I had to regain my wife's respect and love. It was time to become a man of integrity and a man of my word. After a good two years of counseling, communication, and reconciliation, Melanie and I worked it out.

I stayed on with World Wrestling Federation until 1993. I left because I knew I had to get out of the after-hours environment. My leaving had nothing to do with the wrestling business. Rather, it had everything to do with what was going on outside the squared circle.

As I tried to regain my wife's love and respect, my move to WCW allowed me to stay in wrestling and get my life in order. During my stint in WCW—1996–1999—my faith in and reliance on God had grown. I found great comfort in the Bible. Since WCW was using me sparingly, I became more and more absorbed by the word of God. I became very vocal about my salvation and told everyone about my faith.

One day, Hal called me. "Hey, Ted, there is a church in the area that would like for you to come and share your story. What do you think?"

"Hal, I don't know. What do you think?"

"Ted, I think you are ready." So I went to the little church in Kentucky and shared my testimony. I explained to the congregation that I thought I had lost it all, but God restored everything. After giving my testimony, there was a snowball effect. By word of mouth, pastors from other churches contacted Hal and wanted me to come to their church and share my testimony. So I did. I also started to speak at elementary and secondary schools to children, teenagers, and young adults about the dangers of alcohol and drug abuse.

HAL SANTOS:

Teddy is growing as a person, so whatever he does is going to grow. He is very healthy mentally and spiritually. His marriage is very healthy and his family respects him. As his spiritual mentor, I have seen Teddy evolve and the Lord is using him. When he speaks, people are very attentive to what he is saying. He does a great job and he is bringing people to the Lord.

He also walks with integrity and he is challenging men to not just grow old, but to be men of integrity as they grow older. I can see the real fruit of his effort—the more he gets the chance to express, share, or challenge men to help their families. And when you get the man right, the rest of the family will be at peace.

The more churches and schools I witnessed at, the more I was called to attend and preach elsewhere. I began to get more versed in the Bible and I kept praying for God to use me as he deemed necessary. I asked God if this was the role that he wanted me to take. The more I preached, the larger the response and turnout. I knew then that my calling was to be a minister. I went to the elders and leaders of my church and shared with them my calling. I began to take classes at the Morrison Heights Baptist Church to satisfy the requirements to attain the necessary credentials to become a minister. On February 27, 2000, I received my certificate of ordination and was ordained as a Baptist minister.

Ministering has become my vocation in life. Since I was a wrestler and part of the wrestling business my entire life, being a minister was the last thing I thought I would be called to do. Nobody was more shocked than me. But now that I have the calling, God is directing my life.

I had and still have some friends and people in the wrestling industry that are skeptics. They have that wrestling attitude that everything is an angle. Some said that I was just using my ministry to make a living and it was all a work. They are wrong; I don't have to justify my ministering to anyone. We are all sinners and I would never pontificate that I am better than anyone else. Actions speak louder than words. Per the King James Bible, Jesus said in Matthew 7:16–20, "You will know them by their fruits. Do men gather grapes from thornbushes or figs from thistles? Even so, every good tree bears good fruit, but a bad tree bears bad fruit. A good tree cannot bear bad fruit, nor *can* a bad tree bear good fruit. Every tree that does not bear good fruit is cut down and thrown into the fire. Therefore by their fruits you will know them."

There isn't a whole lot of money in being a genuine minister. Regardless of the Million Dollar Man gimmick, I didn't go into the business rich nor am I independently wealthy today. I may be rich in Jesus, but I still have a mortgage, car payments, and bills to pay like anyone else.

STEVE KEIRN:

Our relationship with each other means so much to me. He is one of my closest friends and we have an unconditional friendship. He is always there for me, and I am always there for him.

At the same time, he has to be one of my top-ten friends that I have ever had as far as a companion and someone that I could lean on or talk to. Our spiritual enlightenment is the same with our walk with the Lord. It was like we were both brought through this education of wrestling and then into our spiritual awakening through the wrestling business.

In this business, you make friends and bond or you are just passing acquaintances. Ted and I bonded. After thirty-five years in the business, I can count my closest friends on my hands, and Teddy is one of them.

Part of what I do as a minister is evangelism. I go to churches, schools, organizations, and even wrestling events proclaiming the gospel. At wrestling shows, I never wrestle. I only make appearances and sign autographs.

At schools, I like talking to the youth about their choices and habits. I stress the dangers of alcohol, drugs, and sex. I warn them of unwanted teen pregnancy and sexually transmitted diseases. I try to use my own personal experiences as a way to illustrate these points.

One of the main reasons I am able to go out and minister is because of my notoriety and success as a professional wrestler. Once again, I have to say thank you to Vince McMahon and WWE, and especially to those who have followed my career. No matter what, all of the pastors and schools who have asked me to speak and address their body know that I am real. They see in me a guy who has been out in the world and has been very successful. I had fame, money, and recognition. But none of it mattered. I was still miserable because

I didn't have salvation. Regardless of the material possessions and fame, there was an emptiness that needed to be filled. The only thing that brought me true inner peace and contentment was the King of Kings and Lord of Lords, Jesus Christ.

Upon my release by WWE in 2006, I went back to work full-time in my Heart of David Ministries. I created the ministry and I chose the name based on the biblical character of David. There is a story where the young David slays the giant Goliath. As David approached Goliath, the giant cursed and insulted him. But he didn't run in fear. David stood strong and said, "You come against me with sword and spear and javelin, but I come against you in the name of the Lord Almighty, the God of the armies of Israel, whom you have defied . . . it is not by sword or spear that the Lord saves; for the battle is the Lord's, and he will give all of you into our hands." As Goliath moved in for the kill, David reached into his sack and slung one of his stones at Goliath's head. He hit a hole in the armor and struck Goliath's forehead. The big man hit the ground. David quickly took Goliath's own sword, killing him, then cutting off his head.

David later became king of Israel, but he also sinfully committed adultery with Bathsheba. When he was confronted about it, he repented and confessed his sin. David took full responsibility for his failings and asked God for forgiveness. He was restored and God said that "he is a man after my own heart."

I personally identify with David and it is my desire to be like him. When I was young, I had a very strong faith in God. But I fell away from it while in the wrestling business. When Melanie confronted me about my adultery, I begged for her forgiveness. I also repented and asked the Lord to forgive me. I was soon restored. I want God to say to me, "Ted DiBiase, you are a man after my own heart."

Throughout my ministering, I have been fortunate enough to see many other wrestlers give their lives to Jesus. Some have even got a calling to spread their message to others from the pulpit and the wrestling ring. Guys like Nikita Koloff, Greg Valentine, Sting, "Dr. Death" Steve Williams, and Tully Blanchard are serving the Lord.

Nikita Koloff is a great friend and was one of the better wrestlers in the business. He was a one-time NWA Heavyweight Champion and was voted in 1987 "the most inspirational wrestler of the year" by the flagship wrestling magazine at the time, *Pro Wrestling Illustrated.* Nikita now serves the Lord. He is an ordained minister and is profoundly involved in missionary work. He travels all over the world, including the continents of Africa and South America. Like me, he preaches at churches and schools. We also do Christian wrestling shows and events together in an effort to bring people to Jesus.

NIKITA KOLOFF:

Having worked for different promotions, Teddy and I never crossed paths in the wrestling ring. We only met a few times through our wrestling travels. We really got to know each other after Teddy's acceptance of Jesus Christ.

It is fascinating how the Lord works. Just as Ted and I had parallel wrestling careers (we both had great runs and reached a plateau within our respective companies), we have parallel careers in the ministry. Just as we did similar things in wrestling, we now do similar things in the ministry. For example, we both go to schools to do school assemblies and to prisons to speak; and we do wrestling crusades. From time to time, we will also tag team with each other and do some events, especially the wrestling crusades. Through these events, we have literally seen thousands of people.

In terms of our friendship, a few years back Ted and I became really close at an Athletes International Conference in Phoenix. This is a yearly Christian conference for college and professional athletes in all sports to attend and get ministered to. It has been going on for twenty-six years and during the four-day conference, athletes spend quality time with each other fellowshipping, learning about the Lord, and living the Christian lifestyle. At this conference, many professional wrestlers have been saved, such as Road Warrior Hawk, Big Boss Man, "Mr. Wrestling" Tim Woods, Luna Vachon, Gangrel, Terry Taylor, and Marty Jannetty. Between Teddy and me, we have been able to impact a lot of wrestlers' lives. One year, we had forty wrestlers and their wives in Phoenix at this conference. Besides Teddy and me, some other wrestlers who are members of this conference include Shawn Michaels, Sting, George "The Animal" Steele, Superstar Billy Graham, "Dr. Death" Steve Williams, and Greg "The Hammer" Valentine. Larry Kerychuk has done a great job organizing this conference and thus helps to bring many athletes to the Lord.

In August of 2007, Ted and I went to Israel. We were both baptized in the Jordan River. We walked where Jesus walked and it was a very powerful visit.

SHAWN MICHAELS:

The Lord has taken Teddy from a wrestler to someone who is preaching the gospel and spreading God's word. His career in wrestling was a building block, so when Ted DiBiase came to the pulpit, people knew who he was, and he could draw from that notoriety to preach the gospel.

When I got saved, Teddy was one of the first guys I called. In our industry, nobody used to talk about Christianity and salvation. I needed to talk to someone who was a wrestler and in the business, but who was also a Christian. Someone who knew where I had trod and who could help me make sense of forgiveness and salvation. I reached out to Teddy to help me find my way and I continue to speak with him. He encourages me and others.

He may not be aware of this, but aside from preaching the gospel and preaching from the pulpit, he also reaches out to the wrestling business by the way he encourages the rest of us.

Ted DiBiase is a man who mastered the wrestling business. He was one of the best workers that I have ever had the privilege of watching in the ring. I went from admiring him as a wrestler to having the honor of admiring him as a strong Christian man, preacher, and Christian brother. He is not ashamed of the gospel. Just like he did in the wrestling business, he continues to persevere and drive through it all. So many of the great aspects that he had in the ring, he now has as a man of God, and I admire him greatly for that.

Every day, it is my aspiration and goal to live for the Lord. To serve Him as well as my wife, children, family, and community. After all the years of taking, it is time to give back. I don't care about being famous anymore. I pray daily and try to stay humble and never become the egotistical self-serving fool that I once was. I want to reach people through my ministry and give what God has given me—to influence people so that they may live a wonderful life and attain salvation and eternal life.

17
CONCLUSION

With the guidance of the Lord, I am growing every day as a minister, husband, father, and human being. I continue to spread the word of God and bring people to Jesus from both the pulpit and the wrestling ring.

Melanie and I are closer now and more intimate than we have ever been. She is my best friend and we share everything together. In her downtime, Melanie works as an interior designer and is very successful in her profession. She continues to be empowered by our family, community, and church.

MELANIE:

Over the years, Ted and I have traveled down some smooth roads and some rocky roads, but I would do it all over again. I wouldn't trade anything for it. Any relationship is hard, even a good one. No matter how bad things seem at the time, it is so much better to endure the trouble that it takes to work through them, and come out on the other side and still have each other. This outweighs any benefits that you think you might get from tossing in the towel too soon.

His celebrity status and profession afforded us the opportunity to travel the world and meet many interesting people. Through it all, he has always been up to task and always gives a hundred percent. He puts his family first and has done everything for us. He has always been a wonderful husband and I love him dearly. I can genuinely say that everything is in place the way it should be.

He is a great father and loves his three boys. Ted may be big physically, but he simply has a huge heart—he is just a big old softy. Our children respect and love Ted and they have the utmost admiration for their father. I am also so very proud and thankful that my boys have a relationship with their father; a close, loving relationship. Now that the boys have gotten older, Ted is their confidant.

Ted is a loving husband and an excellent father. He is a servant of the Lord and overall a wonderful human being. Ted cares for others and treats them with dignity and respect. He is simply a great guy and by marrying Ted I hit the jackpot.

I am very proud of my three sons. They have seen me evolve as a father and as a person. We have an excellent relationship. It is funny, however, that the one thing my dad didn't want me to become when I grew up was a professional wrestler. It wasn't because of the actual wrestling, but rather the hardships that came with the business. As the father of three boys, I understand now what my dad was talking about.

While they were growing up, I told my boys that even though there were no guarantees in life, there had to be other professions for them to pursue besides wrestling. "Guys, the hardships of the business and the long hours away from your family isn't worth it. Go to college and get an education so you can attain a stable career. Find a position that will afford you the opportunity to spend quality time with your wife and children." As I write this, however, there is a good chance that there will be three more DiBiases in the wrestling industry.

My oldest son, Michael, is going on thirty. Although he is having a hard time finding out who he is, he is currently focused and is training with Harley Race to become a professional wrestler. Until he tore his anterior cruciate ligament (ACL), he was progressing nicely. I am confident that once he rehabs his knee, he will be back in the ring.

MICHAEL:

How many kids get to grow up watching their hero on TV, and call that hero Dad? Growing up, I always knew the exact time I could turn on the TV and watch my hero. Although what every other kid in the neighborhood thought was the perfect life was not always so perfect.

My brothers and I did not get to see Dad much. He would be gone ten to fifteen days at a time and home for three. His tours to Japan would last usually a month at a time. When he was home, Dad was exhausted from the long road trips. He would come home, change into his red or blue All-Japan sweats, and crash into his recliner. The bottom line was when Dad got home, he was worn out. He only had a few days to recover, spend time with his wife and kids, and get ready to go again. It was a routine we were all used to. It was all we knew.

There are many fond memories that I will always hold close that only a wrestler's kid would understand. I loved going to the shows with Dad. My brothers and I would often take turns going on the road for a few days. At an early age we learned the routine: wake up, catch a plane or get a rental to the next town, check into the hotel, get a bite to eat, get a workout in (if you could find a gym), take a short nap, and be at the arena at least an hour or two before the show started. And if it was TV, you were there all day.

Funny as it may seem, to this day, I remember certain smells: airports, hotel lobbies, Dad's gym bag (where he kept his gear and at times championship belts), and Dad's scent after the matches (a mix of Drakkar cologne and sweat—it seemed that he would never stop sweating). My favorite smell was of the arena. When you first arrived it was cold and quiet. There were a few people bustling around in preparation for the show. I remember roaming around, checking out the venue, watching the guys set up the ring, and listening to the boys talk about their matches. As the night went on and the fans filled the arena, the air would get a little smoky. There was the smell of fresh popcorn popping. The lights would dim with the beginning of the first match. The crowd would go up and down, depending on how well the boys were working that night. Naturally, my favorite part of the night was watching Dad. The one thing I will always remember was no matter the size of the venue or how many people attended, Dad was always the same.

Teddy is twenty-five and a college graduate, with a bachelor's degree in business administration. Although he's had job offers, he is now training to be a professional wrestler. He trained for a year with Harley Race and did two Japan tours. Teddy is now in the WWE developmental program in Tampa. I hear he's "a chip off the old block."

Teddy recently hit the nail on the head when he saw that I was discouraged about him entering the world of professional wrestling. He pulled me to the side and made me proud. "Dad, I did everything you asked me to do. I went to college and got a degree. But the one thing you have to understand is that you have always been my hero. I've always wanted to be like you."

TEDDY:

I don't really know where to start. I really could write an entire book on the influence that my father has had on me. I guess I'll start with something that my father has been telling me for a while now, at least since I've begun approaching manhood and especially now as I am pursuing a dream and a profession in the wrestling business. Dad always said to me, "Son, success is not measured by wealth, possessions, or even fame. It is measured by what kind of man you become. You are either a man of character and integrity, or you're not." My father has been very adamant about teaching me that, in his words, "Wealth and fame can be taken from you in an instant, but who you are as a man and what you stand for is something that no one can take." This is my father and the man that he has become. This is the man that I look up to and admire, and I hope to emulate one day.

My dad has always supported us boys with anything that we set out to do—most of which was football and soccer, and yes, now finally, even wrestling. Just for the record, this was not always the case. He would always say, "Well, if you want to wrestle, then you have to beat me first."

Dad has finally come around and realized that I just want to be a part of the family history: the DiBiase wrestling history. He wanted to be like his dad, and I want to be like mine. He also had to eat his own words: "Don't let anyone tell you that you can't do something!" I really liked bringing that one up when we would argue about me wanting to wrestle. He did make me finish college first, for which I am grateful. This is one thing that he didn't do, but he assured me that he would have if his father had still been alive.

Dad made sure that when we committed to do something, we followed through with it all the way. I played soccer and football. The soccer team that I played on was a select team. We traveled all over and played just about year-round. There were many times when I was younger that I would get burnt-out and just want to quit, so I could have my weekends free to hunt or hang out with my friends. It was these times that Dad used to teach me about hard work, sacrifice, and commitment. I can hear him now: "Boy! You aren't quitting! You made a commitment to your coach and teammates. You're going to finish what you started and that's final!" He always told me stories about how hard his dad pushed him because he told his dad that he wanted to be the best. Well, I wanted to be the best too, and even though he couldn't be at practices or games most of the time because he was on the road, I knew he would be calling, asking for a report on how I did. I've always wanted to make him proud. He never expected me to be the best, he just expected my best. "Make the sacrifices necessary, work hard, and do your best." I've heard those words from him a million times.

My dad has spent his life serving others. If he wasn't entertaining thousands of people in the ring, he was at home washing clothes, doing the dishes, or just doing what he could while he was home to help out my mom. He loves my mom very much, and he should, because she has been there through the good and the bad! He's a lucky man to have such a wonderful wife and I am the luckiest son of all to have her as a mother and him as my father.

My father was a great wrestler and entertainer. I know that, and I am proud of his accomplishments. I can only hope to be as good as he was one day, but I am even more proud that being a good wrestler and entertainer are not his greatest qualities. Unlike for many who have pursued it, the business did not define my father. He's a man with a servant's heart. He has compassion for people in need. He puts God and his family first, before anything else, every day when he wakes up. He's a good husband, and he's the greatest father a son could ask for. I love you, Dad. Thank you for everything.

My youngest son, Brett, is the ham of the family. He is twenty and is a sophomore in college on a soccer scholarship. He isn't sure what he wants to do yet, but I have a feeling that he will be following in his brothers' footsteps. I told Brett and all my boys, as well as kids everywhere I go, "Dream your dream." If you are willing to pay the price, like the Million Dollar Man would say, then you can be anything you want. Don't let anybody tell you that you can't. Be brave enough to live your own dream, not somebody else's dream.

BRETT:

As a kid, I never really figured out that my dad was the Million Dollar Man. To me, he was just my dad. I can't exactly recall when I realized that he was a pretty big deal around the world and to a lot of people. But I do remember thinking that Dad was a big-time wrestler and it was really cool!

Like my two older brothers, as I got older, I was very much into wrestling. I would always go crazy watching Dad on TV, and would yell and beat up my World Wrestling Federation Million Dollar Man daddy doll. While I watched my dad on TV, it bothered me how mean he looked and how he was always cheating. My mom would always try to figure out how to explain to me that my dad was really not a mean guy or a guy that cheated in real life.

One of my wrestling memories with Dad was when I went on the road with him. One time, I met Skinner (Steve Keirn) when he was out of character. He was a great guy and was very nice to me. Later that night, I saw him wrestle in his character with a knife and spitting tobacco out of his mouth. I was terrified. After seeing that, I wouldn't get anywhere close to him.

Although I thought it was cool that my dad was a wrestler, having him just as my dad was even better. Dad raised me in a way that will help me succeed in life. I will never forget when Dad sat me down and said, "Son, there are three things in life that if you abide by them, I won't have to beat you!" He said, "Don't cheat, lie, or steal."

Those things were the same three things his dad, "Iron" Mike DiBiase, had told him.

Let me share a story of how Dad was just being Dad—not the Million Dollar Man, walking around stuffing hundreds in people's mouths. One day, I was in the kitchen and my mother and I were arguing. Now, my brothers and I were never supposed to be disrespectful toward Mom, because that was one thing that would make Dad knock you out. During this argument, Dad walked in and saw what was going on. Well, I raised my voice and Dad popped me right in the mouth. Dad always had a good jab, but when he nailed me this time, out of instinct, I pushed him in his chest. Before I even realized what I had just done, Dad immediately picked me up by my shoulders, with my feet six inches off the floor, and lectured me for about five minutes without ever setting me down. He then tossed me on the couch, opened the door to the backyard, and said, "Come on. Since you think you can hang with me, let's finish this in the backyard like men!" Let's just say I tucked in my head like a dog that had been beaten for peeing on the floor. Dad raised me and my brothers to respect not only our parents, but people in general.

Dad will always be the greatest influence in my life. I want to make him proud with whatever I end up doing with my life. I know if I will use the skills and values he has instilled in me, then I will be able to reach all my goals and fulfill all my dreams. Thanks for everything, Dad. I love you.

I have always respected and valued the wrestling business. It has given me so much, both good and bad. Because of these treasured experiences, I have been blessed with a great and loving wife and family. It has even helped propel me to my current calling with my Heart of David Ministries.

Through it all, I was and always will be extremely appreciative of the fans who came out to cheer but mainly boo me. Without the fans, there is no professional wrestling. I will forever be thankful for the wonderful memories and those who paid the price for me to be part of the greatest industry on the planet.

ACKNOWLEDGMENTS

There are so many people that I want to thank for this project. First and foremost, I want to thank my Lord and savior, Jesus Christ, for apart from him I am nothing, and my wife, Melanie, and my sons, Michael, Teddy, and Brett. I also want to thank the fans, because without them, this story wouldn't have been possible.

Tom would like to thank his wife, Janet, and son, Dante, for all their patience and understanding with the writing of this book. Without Janet's hours of assistance, this book would not have been possible.

Tom and I both wish to thank all the wonderful people at WWE and Pocket Books for their support, especially Dean Miller and Margaret Clark, respectively.

We both deeply appreciate those who took time out of their busy schedules to contribute to the book, including my brothers, John and Mike; Oscar Nanfito; Terry Funk; Bill Watts; Bruce Prichard; "Hacksaw" Jim Duggan; Jim Ross; Harley Race; Michael Hayes; Steve Keirn; Arn Anderson; Mike Rotundo; Terry Taylor; J.J. Dillon; "Dr. Death" Steve Williams; Shawn Michaels; Bob Geigel; Pat Patterson; Bobby Heenan; Nikita Koloff; Tito Santana; Tully Blanchard; Hal Santos; and Mike "Virgil" Jones.